Spencer Watkins, Francis F. Field

The Up-to-Date Cook Book of Tested Recipes

Spencer Watkins, Francis F. Field

The Up-to-Date Cook Book of Tested Recipes

ISBN/EAN: 9783744790031

Printed in Europe, USA, Canada, Australia, Japan

Cover: Foto ©Lupo / pixelio.de

More available books at **www.hansebooks.com**

THE
UP-TO-DATE COOK BOOK
OF TESTED RECIPES.

COMPILED AND PUBLISHED BY

MRS. SPENCER WATKINS

AND

MRS. FRANCIS F. FIELD.

FOR THE BENEFIT OF

St. John's Church,

MONTGOMERY CO., MD.

WASHINGTON, D. C.:
NATIONAL PUBLISHING CO.
1897.

INDEX.

	Page
1. SOUPS.	5
2. FISH, CRABS, ETC.	13
3. OYSTERS.	19
4. MEATS.	25
5. MEAT AND FISH SAUCES.	29
6. POULTRY AND GAME.	35
7. ENTREES.	39
8. EGGS.	48
9. VEGETABLES.	51
10. BREADS.	61
11. SANDWICHES.	69
12. CUBAN RECIPES.	73
13. SALADS.	75
14. PIES AND PUDDINGS.	81
15. PUDDING SAUCES.	93
16. DESSERTS.	98
17. CAKES.	113
18. PRESERVES, PICKLES AND CATSUPS.	129
19. BEVERAGES.	135
20. CANDIES.	141
21. MISCELLANEOUS.	147
22. THINGS WORTH KNOWING.	150

SOUPS.

POTATO SOUP.

Twelve potatoes pared and grated, one onion sliced, one tablespoonful of parsley, one cup unskimmed milk or cream, two tablespoonfuls of butter, one tablespoonful of corn starch wet with cold milk, one teaspoonful of sugar, two quarts boiling water, pinch of soda in milk. Parboil the potatoes ten minutes, throw off the water, and put them into two quarts of boiling water, cook in this one hour, with the onions, replenish from the kettle as it boils away, then set through a fine colander. Season with pepper, salt and parsley, reheat and when it bubbles up stir in the butter and corn starch, boil up, add milk and serve.

MRS. N. B. FUGITT.

TOMATO SOUP.

To one pound of canned tomatoes or four large ones cut fine add one quart of boiling water and let boil till done. Then add nearly a teaspoonful of soda, when it foams add one quart of sweet milk, pepper, salt and butter, or one cup of sweet cream instead of butter, a few cracker crumbs rolled fine, and serve.

MISS SKILES.

CREAM OF CELERY.

One head of celery, one pint water, one pint milk, one tablespoonful butter, one tablespoonful of flour, one-half teaspoonful salt, one-half saltspoonful white pepper. Wash and scrape celery, cut into half-inch slices, put into the pint of boiling water and cook until very soft, when done mash it in the water in which it is boiled and add salt and pepper. Cook an onion in the milk and with it make a white sauce with the butter and flour, add this to the celery and strain through soup strainer, mashing with the back of a spoon until all but a few tough fibres of the celery are squeezed through. Return soup in double boiler to the fire, heat till steaming, when it is ready to serve. MISS SKILES.

VEGETABLE SOUP.

Before breakfast wash a beef shank in several waters, break the bone and put in a large pot of cold water, keep it steadily boiling until one hour before dinner, when the following vegetables previously prepared must be added to the soup, after it has been carefully skimmed of all grease and strained: One pint of peeled and chopped tomatoes, one pint of lima or butter beans, one pint of grated corn, one pint of chopped cabbage, one pint of sliced white potatoes, one sliced turnip, one carrot, little minced onion, parsley, one tablespoonful of pepper sauce, one heaping tablespoonful of flour rubbed into one teacupful of milk, one teacupful of brown sugar, one teaspoonful of black pepper. Boil an hour, thicken with mixed milk and flour and serve.

MRS. WATKINS.

CLAM CHOWDER.

One dozen Little Neck clams, three large potatoes, one-half pound butter, two onions, two tablespoonfuls flour, pepper, salt and one teaspoonful minced parsley, mince the clams fine and boil tender. Put butter and flour in a saucepan, when drawn add clams and about two quarts of the juice, add potatoes and onion, cut fine and cook till done, add parsley, season to taste and serve.

ST. GERMAINE.

CREAM OF CORN.

To each quart of corn cut from the cob (or canned corn) add three quarts of water, boil till tender and then add two ounces of butter that has been well mixed with a tablespoonful of flour, boil fifteen minutes more, season to taste and just before serving add heaping cupful of whipped cream.

MRS. SPENCER WATKINS.

BOUILLON.

Heat clear soup stock, add pepper, salt, celery salt, cloves, a little catsup or Worcestershire sauce, port or sherry to suit the taste. Serve in cups for breakfast or luncheon. When used for dinner call consomme and serve in soup plates. Egg dice, bread dice and force meat balls are put in the tureen and the hot soup is poured over them. Of course, only one kind is used at a time.

MISS HOGE.

DELICIOUS TURTLE SOUP.

Scald and scrape outer skin off the shell of the turtle, open carefully so as not to break the gall, break both shells to pieces and

SOUPS.

put in the pot, lay the fins, eggs and some of the more delicate parts by and put the rest in the pot with a couple of quarts of water, add two onions, parsley, thyme, salt and pepper, cloves and allspice to suit taste. An hour before dinner take the parts laid by, rub them in browned flour, fry them in butter and put with the eggs into the soup. About one-half hour before dinner thicken the soup with browned flour and butter rubbed together. Serve very hot. MRS. SPENCER WATKINS.

CREAM OF CHICKEN.

One three-pound chicken, one-quarter pound butter, one onion, three tablespoonfuls flour, one quart milk, salt, pepper and a little nutmeg, yolks of three eggs. Boil fowl till tender, put butter in pan and work well with flour, then add broth of chicken, which will make a very fine cream, when hot add milk and color with the yolks of eggs. Season to taste and strain through fine sieve. "THE WINDSOR."

OKRA SOUP.

Cut okra in very thin slices and throw into one and one-half quarts of boiling water, when tender add one quart of milk, a large tablespoonful of butter, two tablespoonfuls of flour and white pepper to taste. This soup must be made in porcelain kettle. MRS. SPENCER WATKINS.

OX TAIL SOUP.

Take two ox tails, an onion, two carrots, two stalks of celery, a little parsley and a small cut of pork. Cut the ox tails at the joints, slice the vegetables and mince the pork. Put the pork, onion and ox tails into a stewpan and fry them a short time. Now put the ox tails and fried onions into soup kettle, with four quarts of cold water. Let simmer for about four hours, then add the other vegetables, with four cloves, pepper and salt; as soon as the vegetables are well cooked the soup is done. Strain it. KENTON COOK BOOK.

GREEN PEA SOUP.

Boil one-half peck of peas in one and one-half gallons water till perfectly done, take out, mash and strain through colander, then pour a little water well boiled over them to separate pulp from hull. Return to the water they were boiled in, chop up one large or two small onions, fry them in smallest quantity of lard not to burn them, add this with chopped thyme, parsley, pepper and salt; just before taking from the fire stir in one tablespoonful of butter. If the soup is too thin cream a little butter and flour to thicken. MRS. WATKINS.

CREAM OF TOMATO.

One dozen ripe tomatoes, one carrot, two onions, six cloves, one-half lemon, salt and red pepper to taste, one tablespoonful vinegar, one-quarter pound butter, three tablespoonfuls flour; cut tomatoes, carrot, onion and lemon in small pieces, put in saucepan with one gallon of water, let it boil down to three quarts, draw butter and flour in saucepan, then pour over the hot tomatoes the broth, which will make a cream. Add vinegar, a tablespoonful of sugar and season. Serve with crotons.

"THE WINDSOR."

TO MAKE CROTONS.

Butter a slice of evenly cut bread, divide into cubes one-third of an inch thick, place these cubes on a tin plate and place on the grate of a moderate oven fifteen minutes; when done they should be a light brown, crisp and brittle; sprinkle in soup just before serving.

MISS SKILES.

RICH BEEF SOUP.

Crack the bones of a good beef shank and put in a pot that holds two gallons, fill the pot with cold water and set on the fire; as soon as it begins to boil set it on the back of the stove where it will boil slowly, skim well and put in the vegetables, one-half pint shelled butter beans, one pint ripe tomatoes peeled, one quart tender okra sliced thin, and one-half hour before the soup is done one pint corn cut from the cob. Soup should boil slowly for six or seven hours. Add salt and pepper to taste where corn is added. Before serving carefully skim off all grease.

MRS. SPENCER WATKINS.

OYSTER SOUP WITH MILK.

Boil one quart of rich milk, season with pepper, salt and a large tablespoonful of butter, then add one quart of oysters and just let it come to the boiling point, and serve.   MISS HOGE.

OYSTER SOUP.

One quart oysters, one pint milk, one blade mace, small piece of celery, one tablespoonful butter, tablespoonful of flour, half teaspoonful salt, and few grains of cayenne. Drain oysters in a colander and wash them by passing through a cup of cold water which drains into the liquor. Lift oysters one at a time and examine for pieces of shell. Cook till oysters become plump, but do not allow to boil, heat liquor and water that has been drained into it till bubbles rise to the surface and then skim off scum that rises. Heat milk, mace and celery in same way, remove mace and celery from the milk and add butter and flour that have been creamed together with a little milk. Cook till it thickens, add oysters and serve at once.　　　　　　　　　MRS. WATKINS.

GUMBO.

Fry a large onion in two ounces of lard until it is quite brown, but not at all burnt. Remove all the onion from the lard; in the same lard fry a chicken which has been cut up and floured, only do not cook it quite done; put the fried chicken in a soup pot, then to the same lard fry one (two quarts better) of okra sliced in small pieces, put the okra in the soup pot with the chicken and pour over this three pints of water, let it simmer one hour, not boil fast, then add one quart of tomatoes chopped fine, season with salt and one green pepper chopped fine, parsley, celery tops, grated corn, tender lima beans, let this cook ever so slowly, with meat, until vegetables and meat are undistinguishable and the whole becomes quite thick; a few minutes before serving add a tablespoonful of butter, remove all bones possible, serve with rice.

For a six o'clock dinner begin your "gumbo" at one p. m. If too thick for your taste add a teacupful of hot water from time to time. Gumbo cannot be made in one hour, it must cook slowly a long time. Gumbo can be made of beef cut in small slices, floured and fried in the same way as chicken, and add any bits of cold ham, chicken or veal you may have.　　　　　MISS WAGNER.

| Next to a Good Menu | AND A GOOD DIGESTION IS **A Good Piano**  OURS IS |

The Leading Piano, Organ and Music Warerooms at the National Capital.

Sanders & Stayman...

PERCY S. FOSTER, Manager

1327 F STREET N. W.

Baltimore Store: 13 N. Charles St.

H. BROWNING   A. MIDDLETON

Browning & Middleton

Dealers in Fine Family Groceries, Wines, etc.

Proprietors and Manufacturers of

608 Pennsylvania Avenue N. W. Washington, D. C.

Browning's Celebrated Stomach Bitters...

INSURE YOUR PROPERTY WITH THE

POTOMAC INSURANCE COMPANY

OF GEORGETOWN.

Chartered by Congress March 2d, A. D., 1831.

W. RILEY DEEBLE, *Pres.*   J. H. BRADLEY, *Sec'y*

HOME OFFICE:
1219 Thirty-Second St., Georgetown, D. C.
WASHINGTON BRANCH:
1319 F Street Northwest.

FISH, CRABS, ETC.

TURBOT.

Steam and pick four pounds of fish. Take one quart of milk, one bunch parsley chopped fine, pepper and salt; when milk is nearly boiling thicken with flour until it is the consistency of thick cream. After taking from fire add two well beaten eggs and one-quarter of a pound of butter. Butter a baking dish, put in a layer of fish, and one of dressing, until the dish is full; sprinkle cracker crumbs on top and bake twenty minutes before serving. This can be served in individual dishes. MISS SKILES.

TURBOT DRESSING.

For four pounds of fish before it is picked use one quart of milk and a little parsley, one-quarter pound of butter, pepper, salt and two eggs; boil milk with salt, pepper and chopped parsley thickened with flour, until it is as thick as soft butter. Take from stove and put in while hot two well beaten eggs and the butter.
MRS. K. W. SKILES.

FRESH CODFISH AU GRATIN.

Boil the cod until tender, cut in pieces and put in baking dish; use same sauce as for cauliflower, cover with bread crumbs and send to oven. MRS. G. T. DUNLOP.

BAKED HALIBUT.

Take a piece of halibut weighing five or six pounds, and lay in salt and water for two hours. Wipe dry and score the outer skin. Set in baking pan in tolerably hot oven and bake an hour, basting often with butter and water heated together in tin cup or saucepan. When a fork will penetrate it easily it is done. It should be a fine brown. Take the gravy in the dripping pan, add a little boiling water. Should there not be enough stir a tablespoonful of catsup, the juice of a lemon and thicken with browned flour, previously wet with cold water. Boil up once and put into sauce boat. KENTON COOK BOOK.

ESCALLOPED SHRIMPS.

One and one-half pints of shelled shrimps, one pint of boiling water, one-half pint of grated bread crumbs, one teaspoonful beef extract, two tablespoonfuls of flour, three tablespoonfuls of butter, one generous teaspoonful of salt, one-eighth teaspoonful of cayenne, one teaspoonful of mustard, one teaspoonful of lemon juice. Dissolve the beef extract in the boiling water. Put butter in a saucepan and beat to a cream. Add flour and mustard and beat until light. Gradually pour the hot liquid on this. Place the saucepan on the fire and stir contents until they begin to boil. Now add the lemon juice and half the salt and pepper and cook six minutes. Season shrimps and stir them into the sauce. Turn the mixture in a shallow escallop dish that will hold about a quart, cover with grated bread crumbs and dot with half tablespoonful of butter broken into little bits. Bake for twenty minutes in a rather hot oven. D.

PICKED CODFISH.

Soak as much codfish as you desire to cook over night. In the morning pick it to pieces and place in a saucepan with cream and some potatoes cut into small pieces. Add butter and salt and let it cook until thoroughly tender. Serve over toast on a flat dish.

SPICED MACKEREL.

Soak half dozen mackerel over night, boil until tender, remove bones and lay in stone jar. Boil one quart of vinegar with one grated nutmeg, three blades of mace and three cloves; pour over fish. Will be ready for use in about two days.

KENTON COOK BOOK.

SARDINES ON TOAST.

Drain the oil from a box of sardines and drain the fishes on brown paper. Cut bread into thin slices a little longer and wider than the fishes. Toast and arrange the fishes one on each slice. Stand in the oven until hot. Scatter lightly with grated Parmesan cheese. Garnish dish with lemon and parsley.

FISH CREAM.

For twenty-five guests take two pounds of halibut, boil carefully and pick apart, then, with wooden spoon, mash until perfectly fine. Add two unbeaten whites of eggs, mix thoroughly and then stir in one pint whipped cream. Add two teaspoonfuls salt, dash of pepper, pack into cutlet or other small moulds, stand in steamer and steam for twenty minutes, turn out on heated dish and pour over them sauce Hollandaise. MRS. RORER.

DEVILED CRABS.

Take meat, eggs and coral of twelve large crabs, put in saucepan with half pound butter, warm well. The juice of one lemon, red pepper and salt to taste, small pinch of mustard and one tablespoonful flour; stir well and just before taking from the fire add yolks of four eggs; mix well and fill shells; sprinkle with cracker meal and a little melted butter and brown. One cup of white wine will add to the above.   "THE WINDSOR."

SOFT CRABS.

Turn up ends of shells and take out dead man's fingers, take off flap and cut out sand bag. Lay in cold water till ready to fry. Dust with flour, put little salt and fry in hot lard.
MRS. SPENCER WATKINS.

CRAB A LA CREOLE.

Put into a saucepan a large piece of butter and four young onions cut into rings, two green chilies chopped fine, one small sliced tomato, salt, black pepper, and a little cayennne; stew gently five or six minutes, then dredge in a very little flour and add a very little good cream. Pick the meat from two crabs, put into the sauce, stew two minutes and serve on toast.

DEVILED CRABS.

To twenty-five cents' worth of crab meat add three eggs, a little bread crumbs, red pepper, salt, butter, one onion grated fine. Mix. Put some butter and lard in frying pan; when hot drop these in like potato cakes.   MORGAN.

LOBSTER A LA NEWBURG.

Split two good sized, freshly boiled lobsters, pick all the meat from shells, cut into pieces about an inch square. Place in saucepan over hot fire with one ounce fresh butter, pinch salt, half saltspoonful red pepper, adding two medium sized truffles cut into dice. Cook five minutes then add one wine glass of Madeira wine, reduce one-half, which will take three minutes. Have three egg yolks in a bowl with half pint sweet cream beaten well together, add to lobster. Gently shuffle for two minutes longer, or until it thickens. Pour into a hot tureen and serve.
DELMONICO.

LOBSTER CUTLET.

One pound lobster meat, half pound best butter, half cup flour, pinch mustard, juice of one lemon, salt, pepper and little nutmeg. Put butter and flour in saucepan and make a drawn sauce. Then add lobster meat and work well. Add mustard, minced parsley, salt, pepper, lemon juice and nutmeg. Let cool, then form in cutlets, bread in cracker meal and egg, fry a nice brown. Serve with cream, tomato or Bernaise sauce. "THE WINDSOR."

COD A LA CREME.

Put into boiling water for ten minutes two pounds of fresh codfish, lift it carefully from the water and pick into large flakes with a silver fork. Put one tablespoonful of butter and one of flour into a saucepan, mix, add one pint of milk, stir constantly until boiling, then add codfish, teaspoonful of salt and one-fourth teaspoonful of pepper, stand over back part of fire until smoking hot. Arrange on the serving dish a neat border of mashed potatoes, fresh over with white of egg, run in the oven just a moment to brown, and then add to the codfish mixture the yolks of two eggs; stand over the fire until it just comes to boiling point; pour it into the center of border; sprinkle over some thinly chopped parsley; garnish the dish with gherkins and radishes, and serve. MRS. WATKINS.

SOFT SHELL CRABS.

Take four pats butter, let it become very hot, then put in four medium sized soft shell crabs, first prepared by removing lungs and washing thoroughly. Add two teaspoonfuls lemon juice. Cook about ten minutes, being careful not to burn. Season with little salt and white pepper. Serve on toast or plain. H. H.

OYSTERS.

BROILED OYSTERS.

Lay large oysters on close gridiron. Cook on one side, then on the other. Season with pepper, salt and melted butter. Serve on squares of toast and garnish with thin slices of lemon.
KENTON COOK BOOK.

PHILADELPHIA FRIED OYSTERS.

Purchase large oysters, drain in a colander and dry one at a time on soft napkin or old linen towel, lifting with the fingers, not with a fork. Season them on both sides with salt and pepper. Beat up an egg in a saucer, and add tablespoonful of boiling water and little salt. Have ready on the baking board plenty of powdered bread or cracker crumbs, well seasoned with salt and pepper. Dip each oyster in the beaten egg and then in the crumbs, being careful that every part is covered with crumbs. Meantime heat the fat in which the oysters are to be fried, and test by dropping in a crumb of bread, which will brown quickly if the fat is hot enough. Lay in six oysters, watch carefully, and when they are of a golden brown tint remove with a skimmer, drain on soft paper, and serve at once. Cook more as soon as the first are served. Oysters should never be fried until it is quite time to send them to table. If there are many to fry they may all be dipped and made ready as much as half an hour before they will be needed. They must then be laid on a clean cloth in a cool place until it is time to fry them.
D.

PICKLED OYSTERS.

For one gallon. Wash oysters and strain liquor through flannel, then cook. Lay oysters on dish to cool. Take two quarts of liquor and one quart vinegar (if too acid add more liquor to suit taste). Put on stove with several blades mace, handful cloves and few allspice; boil couple of minutes. Take off, add little cayenne and pour over oysters. Let cool before putting in sealed jars.
MRS. ALPHEUS MIDDLETON.

STEAMED OYSTERS.

Lay some oysters, in the shell,, on a steamer. Set over pot of boiling water until the shells open. Serve at once with salt, pepper and butter. Lemon can also be used.

MRS. ROBINSON.

OYSTER CHARTREUSE.

One quart oysters, one pint cream, one small slice of onion, half cupful milk, whites of four eggs, two tablespoonfuls butter, salt, pepper, two tablespoonfuls flour, one cupful of fine, dry bread crumbs, six potatoes, one tablespoonful minced parsley. Pare and boil potatoes, mash fine and light, add milk, salt, pepper, one tablespoonful of butter, whites of eggs beaten to stiff froth and the parsley. Have a two-quart charlotte russe mould well buttered and sprinkle the bottom and sides with bread crumbs (there must be butter enough to hold the crumbs). Line mould with the potato and let stand a few minutes. Put cream and onion on to boil, mix flour with little cold cream or milk (about one-quarter of a cupful) and stir into the boiling cream. Season well with salt and pepper and cook eight minutes. Let the oysters come to a boil in their own liquor, skim them and drain off all juice. Take the onion from the sauce and add oysters. Taste to see if seasoned enough, and turn into mould very gently, cover with the remainder of potato, being careful not to put on too much at once. When covered bake a half hour in hot oven. Take from oven ten minutes before dishing time and let it stand on the table. It should be baked half an hour. Place a larger platter over the mould and turn both dish and mould at the same time. Remove mould very gently. Garnish dish with parsley and serve. Every part of the mould must have a thick coating of mashed potato, and when the covering of potato is put on no opening must be left for sauce to escape.

KENTON COOK BOOK.

GRILLED OYSTERS.

One dozen large oysters, dry them on a towel, take two large tablespoonfuls of butter, brown slightly in a stewing pan, and when the oysters are thoroughly dry put them in the butter, into which add a small quantity of flour. Let them simmer about twenty minutes, season with black and red pepper, salt and a little Worcestershire sauce. "THE GRAFTON."

OYSTER LOAF.

This is particularly nice when something out of the ordinary is desired for a luncheon. Cut a long loaf of bread into slices about two inches thick. Trim off the crust, make the slices square and then dig out the crumb at the center of each, leaving sides and bottom to form a sort of box. Brush the hollowed squares of bread with melted butter and place them in a quick oven. When they have browned nicely fill them with creamed oysters and serve. D.

CREAMED OYSTERS.

Dry one pint of oysters on a napkin, spread on a plate and season with salt, pepper and a suspicion of cayenne. Make a sauce with one pint of cream, one tablespoonful butter and two of flour. When sauce is cooked roll in the oysters, put in individual scallop dishes and bake in hot oven ten minutes. Mix oysters and sauce while hot and put in oven immediately. "THE WINDSOR."

OYSTER PIE.

One quart of oysters, one pint of milk, one-half pint water, one-half cupful of butter. Put milk, water and butter on stove and let get scalding hot, add one heaping tablespoonful of flour rubbed smooth in a little milk, and cook until it thickens. Add three eggs well beaten, then two tablespoonfuls of rolled cracker and the oysters and let scald, stirring all the time. Season with pepper and salt. Turn this into baked crust. For crust, make after rule for puff paste, line the baking dish and bake. Cut upper crust to fit dish and bake on heavy paper if you haven't pan the right size. Prick bottom crust with fork to prevent blistering.
KENTON COOK BOOK.

PANNED OYSTERS.

Drain oysters in colander. Have a frying pan very hot, pour in the oysters, a lump of butter size of an egg (for a pint of oysters), one tablespoonful cracker crumbs, teaspoonful lemon juice, salt and cayenne pepper. Let all cook together for a minute or so, just until the oysters commence to curl. MRS. INNES.

MINCED OYSTERS.

Chop one quart of oysters, mince one onion fine, add about as many brown bread crumbs as oysters, season with pepper and salt, a little lemon juice with yolks of four raw eggs, one tablespoonful of butter. Cook a little, fill shells and bake a light brown. MRS. J. N. MITCHELL.

OYSTER LOAF.

Cut an oblong slice from the upper side of a Vienna loaf of bread, then scoop out the crumbs from the inside of the loaf. Spread the casing with butter, fill with raw oysters, about a quart; add one tablespoonful of chopped parsley, half a cupful of cream, some small bits of butter, pepper, salt and two drops of Tabasco sauce. Put on the upper crust, put in a baking dish and pour the oyster liquor over it. Cover and bake twenty minutes, basting often with the oyster liquor. When done put on an oblong dish, cut in slices and serve hot. MRS. WATKINS.

FOR Edge Grain Flooring...

2-in., 2½-in. and 3-in. face—Difficult sizes of Georgia Pine Timber — Estimates of cost of Lumber and Mill Work—Go to

Thos. W. Smith
CAPITAL PARK MILLS
1ST AND G STS. N. E.

Headquarters for Building Supplies.

Cook Bros. & Co.

DEALERS IN

Groceries, Fruits and Provisions

1908 and 1910 14th Street N. W., Washington, D. C.

CREAMERY BUTTER A SPECIALTY

Do You Suffer with Headache?

Only one quality lens—the best

A LARGE percentage of chronic cases of headache are the result of eye troubles In such cases instant relief follows the adjustment of the proper glasses. If you have tried medicine without success let us fit you with proper glasses. No charge for examination. Best glasses for the least money. Our business is conducted with a view of securing permanent, not temporary custom. Satisfaction is guaranteed.

McAllister & Feast, Opticians—1311 F St.

Optical Goods, Cameras and Photographic Supplies.

MEATS.

ROAST PIG.

The pig should not be under four or six weeks old. Stuff with cooked sweet potatoes in which a small slice of bacon has been chopped fine, pepper and salt to taste. Scald the pig on the inside, rub with pepper and salt, fill and sew up. Bend the forelegs under the body, the hind legs forward under the pig and skewer to keep in position. Place in a large baking pan and pour over one quart of boiling water. Baste often. When of a fine brown cover the edges of a large dish with curled parsley; first sift over the pig powdered crackers, then place it kneeling in a green bed. Place in the mouth a red apple. If eaten hot serve with the gravy. It is better cold served with little mounds of grated horseradish in the green bed. The mouth must be kept open with a corn cob or piece of wood while cooking.

MRS. CALLAHAN.

BROILED HAM.

Cut in slices; if salty, pour boiling water over the meat and let it stand five or ten minutes. Wipe dry and boil over a clear fire. Pepper before serving. If the ham looks dry, pour a little melted butter on it.

BOILED FRESH TONGUE.

Wash well and put into boiling water to cover, with three tablespoonfuls of salt and one tablespoonful of pepper. Cook six hours or until very tender; cook down in kettle, being careful that it does not burn. Peel off the skin while hot.

KENTON COOK BOOK.

FRICASSEE OF COLD MEAT.

One and one-half pints of cold meat, one pint of water, three tablespoonfuls of butter, one and one-half teaspoonfuls of salt, one-third teaspoonful of pepper, two tablespoonfuls of flour, one teaspoonful of onion juice. Have the meat cut in generous slices. Season it with a teaspoonful of salt and half that much of pepper. Put the butter in a frying pan and set on the fire; when it becomes hot add the flour and stir until smooth and brown, then draw back to a cooler place and gradually add the water, stirring all the time. Put the pan back on the hot part of the stove and season the sauce with the remaining salt, pepper and the onion juice. Simmer for five minutes, then add the cold meat and cook gently for three minutes if it be rare beef, mutton or game; but if the meat be veal or poultry it may cook longer. D.

TO FRY TRIPE.

Cut tripe, if it has been boiled, into strips about four inches wide and six inches long; make batter with eggs, one teacupful of flour and a little milk; pepper tripe and roll in batter. Fry in pan of hot lard; as soon as one side is done turn on other.
MRS. SPENCER WATKINS.

STEWED TRIPE.

Cut one pound of beef tripe into small pieces, stew gently for twenty minutes, drain and add one pint of the tomato sauce. When boiling, serve. D.

VEAL SCALLOP.

Chop some cold roast or stewed veal very fine, put a layer in the bottom of a buttered pudding dish and season with pepper and salt. Have next a layer of cracker crumbs, sprinkle with bits of butter and moisten with a little milk, then more seasoned veal and then another layer of cracker crumbs. When the dish is full wet with gravy or broth. Have a layer of crackers on top wet with milk and two beaten eggs. Bake from half to three-quarters of an hour. Do not get too dry. KENTON COOK BOOK.

FOWL SAUTE WITH GREEN PEAS.

Remnants cold fowl, one and one-half ounces of butter, one dessertspoonful flour, pepper, salt, good pinch of sugar, one and one-half pints peas, one-half pint stock. Cut meat from bones in neat pieces. Put butter in pan and fry fowl to nice brown, having seasoned with pepper and salt, dredge flour over it, stir ingredients well, add peas and stock and stew till peas are tender; put in pinch of sugar. Serve very hot with peas in center.
MRS. SPENCER WATKINS.

FRIZZLED BEEF.

Have the dried beef cut in knife blade slices, shaving as thin as possible. Place it in a frying pan with enough cold water to cover it, set it on the fire in a moderate heat and when steaming well (but not boiling) pour off this water, return the meat and pan to the stove and heat gently, stirring constantly until the beef is somewhat dry, add a tablespoonful of butter to every half pound of beef, stir and cook until the meat curls and is getting slightly crisp, then add sufficient milk for a dressing for the beef, about one cupful. Moisten half a tablespoonful of flour in a little cold milk and when smooth and the milk in the pan is hot add this mixture. When about as thick as cream serve on hot platter.

D.

CREAMED DRIED BEEF.

For a family of six allow one-half pound of beef, two cupfuls of milk, two tablespoonfuls of butter, two teaspoonfuls of flour. Place the beef in a frying pan, cover with cold water, set on the fire and gradually heat to scalding. Drain and return to the stove, stirring and shaking the beef in the pan to dry off all the water. When this is done add the butter to the beef and cook until brown, generally four minutes, stirring all the time. Add the flour to the fat, stir well, cook one minute, then add the milk. It will thicken quickly and should form a creamy dressing for the beef when done. Dust lightly with pepper when on the serving platter.

D.

BEEFSTEAK FRIED WITH ONIONS.

Prepare steak as for broiling, pepper and roll in flour and fry in lard, remove steak from pan when done, add to gravy one chopped onion, pepper, salt, one-half teacupful of water and little mustard. Cook few minutes, put steak in gravy and serve.

MRS. SPENCER WATKINS.

BRISKET OF VEAL.

Get a loin roast of veal, make a dressing of bread crumbs, butter, salt, pepper and thyme or sage, and a little chopped pickled pork. Put this dressing on the under part of the veal and roll. Tie with a strip of muslin. Put into a pan with a little hot water and bake, basting often. Cook a six-pound roast from one and three-fourths to two hours. Make gravy as for roast veal.

MISS HOGE.

ROAST MEAT IN TOMATO.

Make one quart of the sauce as directed. Slice roast beef or lamb thin, as for the table, and just before serving place it in the boiling sauce. Cook just long enough to heat the meat and serve. The secret of making an inviting dish of already cooked meat is not forgetting that it is cooked enough. It should be only heated through.

D.

MEAT AND FISH SAUCES.

CHUTNEY.

Four pounds of brown sugar, one pound of salt, six ounces of powdered ginger, seven ounces of onions, forty large unripe apples, two pounds of Sultana raisins, one-half pound powdered mustard, seven ounces of garlic, two ounces of cayenne pepper, six quarts of vinegar. Peel and chop fine the apples. Boil down. Then mix the other ingredients and add them. Stir well.
MRS. M. C. D. JOHNSON.

CHILI SAUCE.

Two dozen large, ripe tomatoes, four tablespoonfuls sugar, four onions, two green mango peppers, four cups vinegar, four dessertspoonfuls salt, two red mango peppers. Scald and peel tomatoes; put all the ingredients together and boil until the mixture thickens. Chop onions and peppers very fine.
MRS. WATKINS.

SHIRLEY SAUCE.

Eight large tomatoes, one green pepper, one tablespoonful salt, one quart vinegar, one tablespoonful cinnamon, four large onions, four tart apples, two pints brown sugar, one tablespoonful cloves, one tablespoonful allspice. Hash all very fine and boil one and a half hours.
MISS FIELD.

TARTAR SAUCE.

Four yolks of eggs, lemon juice, oil, little vinegar, pickle and parsley chopped fine.
"THE LOSEKAM."

MUSHROOM SAUCE.

Roll piece of butter as large as an egg in heaping teaspoonful sifted flour, stir in two tablespoonfuls warm water, let simmer, pour in one teacupful cream and stir, throw in one pint young mushrooms washed, picked and skinned. Add pepper, salt, another small piece butter, let boil up once shaking pan well and serve.

NASTURTIUM SAUCE.

Stir into one teacup drawn butter, three tablespoonfuls pickled nasturtiums, adding little salt and pepper. Let simmer and serve.

OYSTER SAUCE.

One pint fresh oysters, scalded enough to plump them, add one tablespoonful pepper, vinegar, little black pepper and salt, pour into sufficient quantity drawn butter and serve.
MRS. WATKINS.

TOMATO SAUCE.

Take tomato catsup, mustard, Tabasco sauce, red and black pepper and juice of lemon, mix thoroughly with a fork; add olive oil. When all is thoroughly mixed stir in vinegar.
MISS SKILES.

APPLE CHUTNEY.

Two teacupfuls chopped apples, two teacupfuls chopped onions, one-quarter teacupful red or green peppers chopped, one pint vinegar and one dessertspoonful salt. Scald and pour over the above hot.
MRS. HOUSE.

CREAM SAUCE.

One pint cream, one tablespoonful flour, salt and pepper to taste. Let cream come to a boil, add flour mixed smooth with little cold cream. Boil three minutes.

CAPER SAUCE.

Make a butter sauce and stir into it one tablespoonful lemon juice, two of capers and speck of cayenne. This sauce is for stewed or boiled fish or mutton.

ANCHOVY SAUCE.

Make butter sauce and stir into it four tablespoonfuls essence of anchovy and one of lemon juice. Best for fish.
KENTON COOK BOOK.

MINT SAUCE.

Pour the grease off drippings of roast lamb, add tablespoonful tomato catsup and some green mint chopped fine.
MISS HOGE.

SAUCE HOLLANDAISE.

Put quarter of a box of gelatine in quarter cup of cold water to soak half hour; put one pint milk over fire, beat together yolks of three eggs with four tablespoonfuls sugar, add these to the hot milk, cook a minute. Take from fire and add gelatine, teaspoonful vanilla, and when cold if you use wine, four tablespoonfuls sherry. This should be about as thick as good cream.

MRS. RORER.

VINAIGRETTE SAUCE.

One teaspoonful white pepper, one-half teaspoonful mustard, one teaspoonful salt, one-half cup vinegar, one tablespoonful oil. Mix salt, pepper and mustard, then very slowly add the vinegar, and after mixing thoroughly add drop by drop the oil.

If you take the meat of a rock fish that has been boiled and allowed to get cold, mince the meat fine and serve on lettuce with this sauce, you will have a delicious salad.

MRS. M. C. D. JOHNSON.

DEVILED SAUCE.

Two pats butter, two teaspoonfuls chopped parsley, one teaspoonful mixed English mustard, two chopped onions and two tablespoonfuls vinegar. After butter is well melted cook two minutes; keep continually stirring. Add one tablespoonful Worcestershire sauce, good pinch salt, some black pepper and little cayenne. Additional mustard and Worcestershire sauce may be added if desired to have it more sharp.

H. H.

J. M. BOGLEY & BRO.

—FINE—

Family ...Groceries

1355 32d STREET N. W.

F. W. Scheele

Dealer in

Choice Meats, Fruits and Vegetables

Butterine a Specialty

1424-26 32d Street N. W.
WASHINGTON, D. C.

Harris & Shafer

••••••••

Jewelers

••••••••

1113 Pennsylvania Ave.

WASHINGTON, D. C.

The Place to Get a Good Luncheon!

DOWN-TOWN shoppers who want a nice, well-cooked luncheon or meal at a very moderate price can gratify their appetite HERE. .. ..
Everything that goes on our table is the very best the markets afford —served properly.
We also serve "regular" Breakfasts and Dinners. Ladies find it especially desirable to take their meals here. Pleasant—quiet —home cooking. Our coffee is famous.

The.. Wilson Cafe

611 Twelfth Street

Just above F

POULTRY AND GAME.

STEWED RABBIT.

Cut rabbit into eight pieces; after cooking in salt and water put in stew pan with slice of pork or bacon and with more than enough water to cover it; when nearly done take out the pieces, strain water in which they have been boiled and return all to stew pan with teacupful of milk, little pepper, salt, chopped onion and parsley; after this boils up stir in heaping tablespoonful of butter in which a tablespoonful of flour has been rubbed. Let boil once more, then serve in covered dish with four hard boiled eggs sliced over it and bread crumbs. The same recipe for squirrel. MRS. WATKINS.

BROILED QUAIL.

Split them at the back, broil, basting them often with butter, over a hot fire. As soon as the birds are done add a little more butter, pepper and salt. Can be served on buttered toast.
MRS. INNES.

ROASTED DUCK.

If the ducks are young they are served rare and are not stuffed. An especially delicious flavor is developed in the cooking if a cup of chopped celery and a half cupful of onion is placed in the body of each bird, removing this flavoring before serving. Full grown ducks should be well cooked, an hour and a quarter is usually sufficient, unless of extra size. They should be basted every ten minutes. D.

ROAST TURKEY.

Proceed with turkey as with chicken, allowing fifteen minutes to the pound. Roast slowly and baste often. It is well to cover the breast with a well greased paper. Stuff the turkey with a dressing made of bread crumbs, seasoned with pepper, salt, butter, onion, thyme or sage. Or mix oysters with the bread crumbs or use oysters only. Another way, add raisins and sage to the bread crumbs and omit onion. MISS HOGE.

WILD DUCKS.

Clean the ducks and stuff the body with a dressing of bread crumbs seasoned with pepper, salt, melted butter, sage and onions or a stuffing of onions alone. Fry the onions brown and season with pepper and salt. Place the ducks in a pan and put about a half pint of boiling water in the pan and baste often. Keep covered. If the ducks are young three-fourths of an hour or one hour will cook them long enough. When the ducks are old they should be steamed an hour and then roasted thirty minutes. If the ducks are not fat lay thin slices of bacon over the breast.

KENTON COOK BOOK.

TO BROIL PARTRIDGES.

Place in salt and water an hour or two before broiling. When taken out wipe dry and rub all over with fresh butter, pepper and salt. First broil under or split side on gridiron over right clear coals, turning till upper side is fine, light brown. It must be cooked principally from under side. When done rub well again with fresh butter, and if not ready to serve immediately put in large, shallow tin bucket, which will keep them hot, without making them dry and hard; when served sift over them powdered crackers browned.

MRS. WATKINS.

SMOTHERED CHICKEN.

Flour, pepper and salt thoroughly spring chickens. Put good sized lump butter in pan and let it get hot on top of stove. Put in chickens, breast downwards and brown, then put in oven for about thirty minutes. Add then a half pint water, cover with pan, cook another thirty minutes, basting occasionally. Let cook with breast down until water is added.

CHICKEN PIE.

Stew chicken until tender, remove it and add to gravy pepper, salt, cream and flour, and let come to a boil. Place in baking dish first, back of chicken, then wings and any other pieces and some small pieces of potato, then pour on some of the gravy. Have ready a rich baking powder biscuit dough, roll out half an inch thick and put over the chicken; add rest of chicken and cover again with dough; cut slit in middle of dough, pour rest of gravy through the slit. Place on top of stove, cover lightly and boil ten minutes. Remove cover and bake in oven half an hour.

KENTON COOK BOOK.

ENTREES.

CHICKEN CROQUETTES.

One chicken boiled and chopped very fine, three pairs of sweetbreads, two pairs of calf brains boiled, one tablespoonful butter, one tablespoonful chopped parsley, one-half onion put on stove and cooked a few minutes, strain and mix with other ingredients. Then put one-quarter pound butter, one-half pint cream, two tablespoonfuls flour, yolks of two eggs well beaten; mix all these on the stove and when it begins to thicken pour it with the chicken, sweetbreads and brains, one-half teaspoonful nutmeg or mace (or both), red pepper and salt to taste. Mix thoroughly; if too thick then thin with a liquor from the chicken; one gill of sherry wine. Set in a cool place two or three hours before making in croquettes. MRS. J. MAURY DOVE.

SALMON CROQUETTES.

Fry an onion, chopped fine in one oz. butter, a golden brown, adding one tablespoonful flour moistened with one-half pint of white stock, stirring constantly until it hardens. Season with one-half tablespoonful salt, scant teaspoonful white pepper, same of cayenne, one tablespoonful English sauce, one-half teaspoonful mustard, one teaspoonful chopped parsley. Stir well. Add two pounds salmon cooked and cut fine, with twelve mushrooms also chopped fine. Cook for thirty minutes. Then put back off hot fire, add four yolks of eggs, stir again for one minute; then let cool. Form into croquettes, roll in bread crumbs and egg and fry in very hot lard. DELMONICO.

RISSOLES.

Roll the trimmings from pie crust into a sheet about one-sixth of an inch thick. Cut this into cakes with the largest patty cutter. Have any kind of meat or fish prepared as for croquettes. Put heaping spoonful on each cake. Brush edges of the paste with beaten egg, then fold and press together. When all are done dip in beaten egg and fry brown in boiling lard. They should cook about eight minutes. Serve hot. MISS HOGE.

CANNELON OF BEEF.

Two pounds of round of beef that has hung for several days,

the rind of half a lemon, four sprigs of parsley, one teaspoonful of salt, one-fourth teaspoonful pepper, quarter of a nutmeg, two tablespoonfuls melted butter, one raw egg and one teaspoonful onion juice. Chop meat, parsley and lemon rind very fine, add other ingredients and mix thoroughly, then add one teaspoonful lemon juice. Shape into rolls about three inches in diameter and six in length. Roll in buttered paper and bake half hour, basting with butter and water. Place on hot plate and serve with tomato sauce. MISS SKILES.

CREAMED TURKEY WITH MUSHROOMS.

One pint of any kind of cold fowl cut in pieces about the size of dice and creamed. Half can mushrooms or same quantity of fresh mushrooms; one tablespoonful flour creamed with tablespoonful butter. Serve in patty shells. MRS. WATKINS.

STUFFED CUCUMBERS.

Halve cucumbers and remove seeds; boil four tablespoonfuls rice for half hour; drain and add to it equal quantity of chopped meat. Peel two tomatoes, halve and press out seeds; cut into small pieces and mix with other ingredients; add half teaspoonful salt and dash of pepper; place this mixture in cavity from which seeds were taken; put halves together; bind cucumbers in shape with piece of twine and stand in baking pan. Add half cupful of water, bake slowly one hour, basting four or five times. These may also be baked by stuffing the mixture into the space from which seeds were taken and baking in halves.

SCALLOPED CUCUMBERS.

Peel four good sized cucumbers, cut into slices and then into blocks. Crumb sufficient bread to make a pint. Cover bottom of baking dish with layer of the crumbs, then layer of cucumbers, and sprinkle over it a tablespoonful of chopped onion, then another layer of crumbs, cucumbers, chopped onion, with a dusting of salt, pepper and celery and having the last layer crumbs. Dot over this a tablespoonful of butter cut into pieces. Bake in a moderate oven one hour. MRS. INNES.

PRESSED CHICKEN.

To one boiled chicken picked as for salad add one dozen olives. Cut up three green peppers, two heads of celery, season with red pepper and salt to taste and mix all well. Take one dozen hard boiled eggs, slice and place them around the bottom and sides of a deep dish, then put the chicken in. Let the liquor in which the chicken was boiled boil down to a pint, then add a quarter of a box of gelatine which, when dissolved and cool, pour on the chicken in the mould. Let it stand until perfectly firm and turn out into a dish. Serve with lettuce and mayonnaise.

ESCALLOPED CHICKEN.

One can mushrooms, two whole eggs or four yolks, one chicken chopped fine with one pair of parboiled sweetbreads. Put on fire, add one pint of cream or rich milk. As it comes to a boil stir in one cup of butter creamed with one tablespoonful corn starch. Stir in eggs well beaten, salt and pepper to taste. Mix chicken and mushrooms, put in baking dish with cracker crumbs on top and bake brown. MRS. J. N. MITCHELL.

DEVILED CHICKEN.

Chop very fine any pieces of chicken that may be left. To every pint of the meat allow one-half pint cream, one tablespoonful butter, one of chopped parsley, three hard boiled eggs, two tablespoonfuls bread crumbs, quarter of nutmeg grated, salt and cayenne to taste. Put butter in a frying pan to melt, add bread crumbs, the cream, chicken and seasoning. Stir over the fire until it boils, then add the hard boiled eggs chopped very fine. Fill paper cases or individual dishes with this mixture, sprinkle lightly with bread crumbs and brown in quick oven.

MRS. BILLINGS.

SWEETBREAD AND MUSHROOOM PATES.

Ten sweetbreads parboiled, skimmed and all fat removed; cut in small pieces. Add one even teaspoonful salt, one can French mushrooms. Slice thin, add to juice one teaspoonful salt, one teaspoonful pepper, one saltspoonful powdered mace, lump of butter size of guinea egg. Simmer slowly twenty minutes, add sweetbreads dredged with one heaping spoonful corn starch, well mixed in sweetbreads. Let boil up once stirring so as to prevent sticking. Serve in pate shells. MRS. WATKINS.

BREADED CHEESE.

One cupful of coarse bread crumbs, three cupfuls of milk, one cupful of grated cheese. Put into pudding dish with crumbs and butter on top. Bake thirty minutes. MRS. INNES.

STUFFED GREEN PEPPERS.

Half loaf of stale bread (not crust) grated. One slightly fried onion chopped fine, one slice boiled ham chopped fine. Fry ham and onion together. One scalded tomato chopped fine and mixed with the above. Mix in the yolk of one egg and a piece of butter size of an egg. Half teaspoonful of powdered thyme. Add bread to make thick paste. Stuff pepper and bake. Serve with tomato or any other good sauce. "THE LOSEKAM."

TERRAPIN.

Six medium sized terrapins, six eggs, half pound butter, one quart cream, salt, pepper and vinegar to taste; add cream last. Boil the eggs hard; cream yolks, pepper, salt and vinegar together. Put terrapin on fire and when boiling add the cream and boil. MISS SKILES.

SPICED BEEF.

Boil shin of ten pounds beef till meat falls from the bone. Pick to pieces, rejecting all gristle. Set liquor away to cool, remove fat, boil liquor to a pint and a half, then return meat to the liquor and while hot add salt, pepper, half teaspoonful cloves, little nutmeg, parsley, cinnamon and a very little sage and savory. Let it boil up once and then pour into a mould or deep dish. Cut in slices. MRS. WATKINS.

CHICKEN TERRAPIN.

Boil a chicken, take off skin and cut up as for salad. Add quarter of a tumbler of cream or milk, put over fire, then add the following dressing: Yolks of three hard boiled eggs mashed fine and add a quarter pound of butter, red and white pepper to taste and one teaspoonful of salt. Mix all well together, and add one wine glass of sherry. When taken off fire add another wine glass of sherry. MRS. TRAPIER.

CREAMED SWEETBREADS.

Parboil pair of sweetbreads; when cold cut up and remove tough parts not to be used. Make sauce of one quart milk, parsley chopped fine, suspicion of onion, teaspoonful of Worcestershire sauce, salt and pepper to taste, three or four tablespoonfuls of corn starch, three tablespoonfuls butter. Boil milk, add butter, pepper, salt and other ingredients and stir in the corn starch. Mix with sweetbreads and put in patty dishes, sprinkle top with buttered crumbs and bake in hot oven for ten minutes.
MISS SKILES.

WELSH RAREBIT.

Melt one pound creamed cheese in one tablespoonful butter, stirring briskly the while. Beat up two eggs, teaspoonful mustard,

pinch red pepper, pinch salt, half bottle ale or beer together and mix with cheese. Cook ten minutes on moderate fire.
"THE GRAFTON."

ORANGE OMELETTE.

The thinly grated rind of one orange and three tablespoonfuls of its juice, three eggs and three teaspoonfuls of powdered sugar. Beat the yolks, add sugar, rind and juice; fold in the beaten whites and cook. Fold, turn out, sprinkle thickly with powdered sugar and score in diagonal lines with clean, red hot poker.
MISS SKILES.

CHEESE CROQUETTES.

Two ounces bread crumbs, two ounces grated cheese, one egg, pepper, salt, cayenne. Mix cheese and bread crumbs well, season rather highly, mix with white of egg, form into balls, dip into beaten yolk of an egg, then into bread crumbs and fry to light brown. Dry on blotting paper and serve. MRS. WATKINS.

TO STUFF GREEN PEPPERS.

Make a white sauce as follows: One tablespoonful of butter, a little more than the same of flour, put on fire and let melt rubbing flour slowly in butter, add two cupfuls milk, stir well; when it thickens take it off, chop one small tomato, parsley, celery tops, very little onion, stale bread, the lean part of a strip of bacon (ham is better), veal, beef or lamb all up together, then add some of the white sauce, perhaps three tablespoonfuls to five peppers, cut peppers from the top, take out all the seeds, then stuff with the above mixture, put on the tops, put in the stove and cook three-quarters of an hour; dust the top with cracker crumbs before putting on the tops. MISS WAGNER.

BRAISED SWEETBREADS.

Three pairs of sweetbreads, two tablespoonfuls of butter, one level tablespoonful of flour, one-half pint of water, one teaspoonful of minced carrot, two teaspoonfuls of minced onion, one teaspoonful of salt, one-quarter teaspoonful of pepper, one-half teaspoonful of extract of beef, one bay leaf, one small sprig of parsley, one small teaspoonful of lemon juice. Clean the sweetbreads and let them soak for one hour in two quarts of cold water into which two tablespoonfuls of salt have been stirred. On taking them from the salt water drop them into a bowl of boiling water for two minutes; then arrange them in a deep baking pan. Put the butter, herbs and vegetables in a frying pan and set on the stove. Cook slowly for fifteen minutes, then add the flour and stir until the mixture becomes frothy. Add the water gradually, stirring all the time. When this liquid boils stir in the meat extract, salt, pepper and lemon juice. Cook for five minutes and strain over the sweetbreads. Cover the pan and put in a moderately hot oven. Cook for one hour, basting every fifteen minutes with the gravy in the pan. Arrange the sweetbreads on a warm dish and pour brown mushroom sauce around them.

HEAD-CHEESE.

Head-cheese (pork) is usually made of the head, ears and tongue, but the head alone may be used if preferred. Clean the meat with the utmost care and boil both the meat and the bones in salted water until the former is very tender. Take out the head, place it in a colander to drain and remove all the bones with a knife. Cut the ears rather fine and place them with the head meat. Season the whole to taste with salt, pepper, sage, sweet marjoram and any other herbs that may be available, and also a little powdered cloves. Mix the mass well together and pack it tightly in a bowl, interspersing layers of the mixture with slices of the boiled tongue. Press the whole into a compact shape and cover it with a plate on which is placed a sufficiently heavy weight. The head-cheese will be ready to use in two or three days. It may be cut in thin slices and served with vinegar and mustard, if liked; or it may be cut in slices, dipped in egg and cracker crumbs and fried. D.

FROG LEGS FRICASSEE.

Take three pats butter and let become thoroughly melted, add little salt and two teaspoonfuls lemon juice or vinegar, put in three dozen medium sized frogs' legs, cover dish and cook for thirteen minutes over open fire, being careful not to burn; remove juice, add one and a half cups white sauce; if too thick thin with some of juice removed. Cook about three minutes, season to taste and serve. H. H.

Have You Seen...

The Woodwork in St. Peters Church? It was all made at Capital Park Mills, including the handsome Hardwood Door and Choir front.

Thos. W. Smith,

1st and G Sts. N. E.   Proprietor.

Everything New   First-class Ladies' and Gents' Restaurant

Morgan House..
EUROPEAN

R. W. MORGAN, Proprietor.   32d St. above M
West Washington, D. C.

"Odd things not found elsewhere."

W. C. Shaw & Co.
Jewelers and Silversmiths

1105 F Street N. W.
Washington, D. C.

Thos. L. Hume

Best Coffee
Pure Spices

Dealer in
Fancy Groceries
Choice Wines
and Liquors

Sole Proprietor of Tunlaw Flour

1204 32d St., Washington, D. C.

B. F. Waddey
HATTER AND FURRIER

3139 M Street

. . .

Dealer in
Gloves, Canes and Umbrellas

Finest Goods
at the Lowest Prices

EGGS.

OMELETTE.

Six eggs, one large teacupful of milk, piece of butter the size of an egg, little pepper and salt and dessertspoonful of flour. Beat yolks and whites separately, melt butter in the milk and stir into the yolks; put the flour in a little of the milk and stir well; add to the yolks lastly the whites beaten to a very stiff froth. Bake in pan well greased with lard in quick oven.

MRS. ALPHEUS MIDDLETON.

STUFFED EGGS.

Boil the eggs hard and cut in two, remove the yolks, mash fine, adding pepper, salt, melted butter and mustard to taste. Fill the cavities and bind the two pieces together. A little chopped parsley can be added or omit the mustard and add a little chopped chicken, in which case roll in egg and cracker crumbs and fry in hot lard.

KENTON COOK BOOK.

EGGS A LA SUISSE.

Butter a dish, put one and a half ounces of grated cheese, then four eggs, not breaking the yolks; two tablespoonfuls of cream, pepper and salt; cover with another one and a half ounces of cheese and bake ten minutes. This may be served one egg in each little saucepan with enough cheese, etc., for itself.

MRS. BILLINGS.

STIRRED EGGS.

Three eggs, one-half pint of milk, one tablespoonful of butter, one-quarter saltspoonful of salt. Place butter in the chafing dish, beat eggs until light, add to them the milk and salt, and when the butter is quite hot stir in this mixture, stirring with a silver fork until the eggs are creamy and cooked sufficiently. Serve on toast.

D.

BREADED EGGS.

Boil hard and cut in round, thick slices. Pepper and salt, dip in beaten raw egg, then in fine bread crumbs or cracker crumbs and fry in hot butter. Serve with cream sauce.

KENTON COOK BOOK.

VERMICELLI EGGS.

Four eggs, one tablespoonful of corn starch, one-half tablespoonful of butter, six squares of toast, one-half pint of milk, salt to taste. Boil eggs for twenty minutes and when cold remove shells, chop the whites fine and rub the yolks through a coarse sieve or a potato strainer. Do not place the yolks with the whites, as they are used separately. Toast the bread a light brown, see that the squares are uniform and without crust, and lay them on the serving platter. Scald the milk and add the corn starch thinned with two tablespoonfuls of cold water or milk. Stir until of the thickness of cream and then add the seasoning and the chopped whites of the eggs. Lightly butter the toast and heap the egg sauce upon the slices. Take a small portion of the powdered yolks and place it on the sauce on each slice of toast, making little nests of it until all is used, and then serve.   D.

EGG BALLS.

Make a thick syrup of one pound of sugar and teacupful of water. Beat the yolks of twelve eggs until very light and almost white. Take syrup off stove and stir in the eggs. Put back on the stove and let it cook slowly until quite thick. After cool roll into balls and dip in caramel as you would fruit glacé. When carameled place in dish one row above the other in a circle, filling in the center with spun caramel.

PICKLED EGGS.

Boil eggs twenty minutes, shell them and place in crock, pour over them spiced vinegar. Will be fit for use in twenty-four hours. If you use vinegar in which beets have been pickled it makes the eggs a pretty color and gives a good flavor.
KENTON COOK BOOK.

VEGETABLES.

TIME TABLE FOR COOKING VEGETABLES.

Potatoes, boiled ....30 minutes
Potatoes, baked ....45 minutes
Sweet potatoes, boiled............................45 minutes
Sweet potatoes, baked.............................1 hour
Squash, boiled ....25 minutes
Squash, baked ....45 minutes
Green peas, boiled.........................20 to 40 minutes
Shell beans, boiled...............................1 hour
String beans, boiled..........................1 to 2 hours
Green corn ....25 minutes to 1 hour
Asparagus ....15 to 30 minutes
Spinach ....15 minutes
Tomatoes, fresh ....1 hour
Tomatoes, canned ....30 minutes
Cabbage ....45 minutes to 2 hours
Cauliflower ....1 to 2 hours
Beet greens ....1 hour
Onions ....1 to 2 hours
Beets ....1 to 5 hours
Turnips, white ....45 minutes to 1 hour
Turnips, yellow ....1½ to 2 hours
Parsnips ....1 to 2 hours
Carrots ....1 to 2 hours

MACARONI A L'ITALIENNE.

Twelve sticks of macaroni, two tablespoonfuls cream, one tablespoonful flour, one-half pint rich milk, two tablespoonfuls butter, salt, white pepper and cayenne, and one-quarter pound of cheese. Wash and boil the macaroni rapidly for twenty minutes in two quarts of water, put the milk on in the double kettle, mix the butter and flour together and stir into the boiling milk, add the seasoning, cream and grated cheese. Drain and dish the macaroni, pour the sauce over and serve immediately. One tablespoonful of mustard may be stirred into the sauce if you desire.

If the sauce and macaroni stand long after being mixed the dish will be spoiled, therefore, if they cannot be served immediately, keep both hot on separate dishes. As it is awkward to serve the macaroni in unbroken sticks some prefer to break the sticks before boiling, but the true Italian way is to serve with unbroken sticks.   MRS. M. C. D. JOHNSON.

TO STUFF EGG-PLANT.

Parboil one or two egg-plants, cut lengthwise, remove all the pulp, beat with two tablespoonfuls of butter until well mashed, add two eggs well beaten, yolks and whites separately; slice stale bread soaked in teacupful of milk, one onion chopped fine, pepper and salt, mix all thoroughly, replace in skins and dust well with cracker crumbs, and glaze with white of egg; bake until a rich brown. Cucumbers, cooked in the same manner, are delicious.
MISS WAGNER.

HASHED BROWN POTATOES.

Place a tablespoonful of butter in a frying pan and when hot add cold, boiled, finely chopped potatoes to the depth of an inch; usually four good sized potatoes will be sufficient. When chopping them add a teaspoonful of salt and a dash of pepper. Press the potatoes down in the pan, packing it firmly with a limber knife; cook slowly for six or seven minutes, when the potatoes should be brown. Do not stir it. Now begin at one side of the pan and fold the potatoes over on the other like an omelette, packing it closely together. Turn it upside down on the serving platter, when ready to serve.

STUFFED POTATOES.

Any cooked meat may be used for this dish. Chop the meat very fine and season it with salt, pepper, a bit of butter and a tablespoonful of tomato, a sprig of celery, parsley or a grating of onion. Cut large sized potatoes into halves, remove the centers, leaving a half inch wall, and fill with the seasoned meat, then put the two halves together, tie with twine, cut off one end of the potatoes, stand them upon their ends in a pan or dish, cover tightly and bake for forty minutes.

CREAMED BAKED POTATOES.

Make a cream sauce of one tablespoonful of butter, one tablespoonful of flour, one-half pint of milk, one-quarter teaspoonful of salt. Rub the butter and flour together until smooth and add it to the milk when boiling; when creamy add the salt. Cut cold, boiled potatoes into small blocks, place them in a baking dish, add salt and pepper and cover with the cream sauce, sprinkle over it a thin layer of bread crumbs and bake until brown.

POTATO OMELETTE.

Four eggs, one ounce of bread crumbs, two ounces of potatoes, one-half ounce of butter. Boil the potatoes and mash them with

VEGETABLES.

the butter, adding the bread crumbs and the eggs well beaten, leaving out one white; season with salt and pepper, fry the omelette in the pan with a little butter and serve very hot.   D.

CREAMED POTATOES.

Bake potatoes in skin till nearly done, let them get thoroughly cold, then cut in small dice; have milk, pepper and butter in saucepan and when hot pour in potatoes, shaking or stirring all the time, which will be only a minute or two. Salt and serve.
MRS. COLLINS.

MINCED POTATOES.

Boil potatoes with skins on until almost done. When cold peel, cut in pieces size of dice, season with cayenne pepper, salt and parsley. Have frying pan with some hot butter in it, pour in the potatoes, press together, cover tightly and cook ten to fifteen minutes, turn out on hot dish with crust up.   MISS HOGE.

POTATO PUFF.

Stir two cupfuls mashed potatoes, two tablespoonfuls melted butter and some salt to a fine, creamy condition; then add two eggs, well beaten separately, and six tablespoonfuls cream; beat all well and lightly together, pile in the dish and grate cheese over top; bake in quick oven until delicate brown.
KENTON COOK BOOK.

CREAMED SWEET POTATOES.

To make creamed sweet potatoes peel cold potatoes left from dinner the night before, cut into blocks and warm in a cream sauce made by beating half cupful of milk in a skillet, then put in one tablespoonful flour rubbed till smooth with one tablespoonful of butter, season with salt and pepper and stir until cooked; then put in the potatoes, allow them to be thoroughly heated and serve.   D.

BROILED TOMATOES.

Cut tomatoes in thin slices, sprinkle each slice with bread crumbs, pepper, salt, and broil eight minutes; put into hot dish and place in oven a few minutes. Small pieces of butter should be put on each slice. Little sugar on each slice may be added.

BAKED TOMATOES.

Take eight or ten large, fine, ripe tomatoes, skin and cut out core. Place in baking pan and fill centers with butter, sprinkle with pepper and sugar, dredge over with flour, pour small cupful cold water in pan; bake half hour in moderate oven.
KENTON COOK BOOK.

STEWED MUSHROOMS.

Peel the mushrooms, scrape the stems, cutting off the hard ends, then wash in cold water. Place in a saucepan a tablespoonful of butter, and when melted add one-half tablespoonful of flour; add one pint of mushrooms, cover and let simmer in a gentle heat for ten minutes, stirring often. Add two tablespoonfuls of cream, heat again, salt and pepper and serve. All stirring should be done with silver spoon; if it turns black they are not mushrooms, but are poisonous, and must be thrown away.

BROILED MUSHROOMS.

Peel the mushrooms and cut off the stalks, heat the broiler, lay the mushrooms carefully in and broil with the upper side first exposed to the fire; then turn and broil the under side. Cook but eight or ten minutes, when they should be tender. Remove from the fire and baste with melted butter, season with salt and pepper and serve on toast.

CREAMED MUSHROOMS.

Drain off the liquor from the mushrooms and place it in a bowl to be used for the sauce. Place on the fire in a granite pan one tablespoonful of butter, heat slowly and add one tablespoonful of flour, stir until they are blended but not in sufficient heat to brown, and gradually add the liquor from the mushrooms and enough cream to make a thin sauce; into this turn the mushrooms, season with salt and when thoroughly hot serve on squares of toast.

OMELETTE OF CORN.

This is a satisfactory way to use boiled corn. Cut the grains from the cob until a cupful is obtained, beat six eggs, yolks and whites together, until light, add six tablespoonfuls of milk and the corn, season with salt and pepper, mixing well. Place a teaspoonful of butter in the frying pan, and when hot add the egg mixture and cook as with any omelette.

CORN OYSTERS.

To one pint of grated corn add one scant half cupful melted butter, three tablespoonfuls of milk, two teaspoonfuls salt and one-fourth teaspoonful pepper; beat well five minutes. Have butter very hot in frying pan, drop batter from spoon and fry until brown on both sides.   KENTON COOK BOOK.

CAULIFLOWER AU GRATIN.

Boil cauliflower till tender, put in earthenware dish whole. Make sauce of half pint of milk, two tablespoonfuls flour and little butter, one spoonful pepper and salt, two ounces grated cheese; pour over cauliflower and bake until light brown.
                                    MRS. GEO. T. DUNLOP.

TO FRINGE CELERY FOR GARNISHING.

Cut the stalks into two-inch lengths, stick plenty of coarse needles into the top of a cork, draw half of the stalk of each piece of celery through the needles; when all the fibrous parts are separated lay the celery in a cold place to curl and crisp.
                                    MRS. M. C. D. JOHNSON.

STEWED CUCUMBERS.

Select rather large cucumbers, peel them, cut into halves lengthwise and then into quarters. Lay them in a shallow pan, cover with boiling salted water and stew gently for twenty minutes. When done lay them carefully on toasted bread and pour over them this sauce: Two tablespoonfuls of butter, one-half pint of boiling water, one-half lemon, one tablespoonful of flour, one-half teaspoonful of salt, a dash of pepper. Place half of the butter in a stew pan, and when melted add the flour. Cook, but do not brown, and when quite smooth add the boiling water. Simmer gently for about ten minutes, stirring all the time, then add the rest of the butter and the seasoning and serve at once.

CUCUMBERS IN MILK.

Cut the cucumbers in small squares after the paring has been removed and place in a saucepan over a slow fire. Add a little salt and water and cook until tender, using only just enough water to keep the cucumbers from burning. Put a pint of milk on the fire and when it boils add two tablespoonfuls of flour which has been made smooth in half a cupful of the milk reserved for this purpose from the pint. When it has the consistency of cream add the cucumbers, drained from their cooking. Sweeten slightly and serve.

CREAM SPINACH.

Use only the tender parts of the spinach, washing thoroughly; this vegetable needs a great deal of cleansing. Place it in a large stew pan, cover with boiling water (salted) and cook for twenty minutes. Drain well and chop fine, then return to the kettle and add one tablespoonful of butter, salt and pepper, stir until thoroughly hot and the butter is melted, then add two tablespoonfuls of cream, beating until the whole is light and creamy.

STEWED OKRA.

Wash a pint of okra, cut it into pieces crosswise, place in a granite stew pan, cover with salted boiling water and simmer gently for half an hour. Add two tomatoes that have been peeled and chopped and stew for ten minutes longer. Add a seasoning of butter, pepper and salt, if more salt is needed.

A preparation of corn, okra, tomato and lima beans affords an appetizing dish for luncheon.   D.

HOT SLAW.

Two eggs, one tablespoonful butter, three of cream, one of sugar, half teaspoonful mustard, pinch of red pepper, little onion and parsley, two tablespoonfuls vinegar; cook until thick, quarter head of cabbage. Pour over cabbage and heat all through before serving. For cold slaw leave out onion and parsley.

MRS. WATKINS.

DRESSING FOR SLAW.

Two eggs, two tablespoonfuls sugar, two tablespoonfuls vinegar, one tablespoonful butter, one teaspoonful mustard, pepper and salt to taste, two tablespoonfuls milk; beat all together and boil until thick, take off and add teaspoonful olive oil, pour over slaw while hot.   MARY BROOKS.

STUFFED ONIONS.

Parboil and cut out the heart of the onions, fill with any kind of meat finely chopped and highly seasoned. When onions are filled put little butter on each, cover with bread crumbs and bake one hour. Serve with cream sauce.

BAKED BEANS.

Wash beans in warm water, put in pot with plenty of hard water and let simmer until they are transparent or begin to sink, then

VEGETABLES.

throw into colander to drain. Put back in pot and pour on boiling water and let come to a boil, place half the beans in bottom of gallon crock, and in center a nice piece of uncooked pork, seasoned with pepper, cover with rest of beans within three inches of the crock and pour boiling water until you can see it between the beans, cover with plate and bake six hours in slow oven. Whenever the water has cooked down so you cannot see it pour on more boiling water; if, when you taste them, they are not seasoned enough, put a little salt in a cup and pour boiling water on it and pour over beans; the last water should not be poured on over half an hour before beans are done. Tablespoonful of molasses can be added. KENTON COOK BOOK.

TO BOIL RICE.

To prepare it cover a cupful of rice with plenty of boiling water, add a teaspoonful of salt and stir often from the bottom so the rice will not stick. Cook for about twenty minutes, when the grains should be quite done but not enough so that they will stick to each other. Drain through a colander, return to the kettle and set uncovered on the back of the range in a gentle heat, shake the kettle often to loosen the rice from the bottom; it will dry in ten minutes so that every grain is quite separate from the others. If cooked a moment too long rice will be too soft and the grains will not dry off. Care should be taken to drain it from the water as soon as all hardness is gone from the center of the grain.

FRIED SQUASH.

The white "button" squashes about four inches in diameter are best when fried. Cut the vegetable into thin slices, dip in beaten egg, then in seasoned bread or cracker dust and fry in hot fat, place a colander in a granite saucepan, lay a soft yellow paper in the colander and as the slices become brown place them on the paper; set the saucepan in the oven or in a warm place on the range; the paper will absorb all of the oil that may be left in the squash. Serve on a platter or other flat dish. Fried squash forms an excellent luncheon dish. D.

HUTTON & HILTON ... Pharmacists
Cor. 22d and L Streets Northwest
WASHINGTON, D. C.

H. W. FISHER & SON
Cor. 32d and N Streets N. W.

DEALER in Choice Fruits, Meats and Vegetables. Fine Provisions. Fresh Fish, Oysters and Game in Season.

JOHNSON & LUTTRELL

Dry and Fancy Goods at popular prices.   713 Market Space

Beall & Baker

Dealers in

Choice Family Groceries

Fine Wines, Liquors and Cigars

Telephone 981
486 Pennsylvania Avenue
Washington, D. C.

The Losekam..

1323 F Street Northwest

FOR FIFTEEN YEARS this has been the Delmonico of Washington for Ladies and Gentlemen. Prompt service and first-class in every respect. Special attention given to parties after the theatre. Ladies shopping will find an elegant lunch served in Ladies' Cafe from 12 to 2:30 P. M. same as business gentlemen's lunch in Gents' Cafe. Private Dining Rooms for three or more persons.

T. R. MARSHALL, Proprietor

Telephone 1188.

BREADS.

PARKER HOUSE ROLLS.

Two quarts flour, one large spoonful lard, small teaspoonful salt, one pint boiled milk, set aside to be cooled, half cupful sugar, half cupful yeast; mix and let rise over night. In the morning knead well and let rise till noon; make into long, narrow rolls, let rise till tea time.

HOT ROLLS.

Mix following ingredients: Four pints flour, one pint fresh milk, two eggs well beaten, one large tablespoonful melted lard, one large tablespoonful hop yeast; set to rise at 11 a. m. for early tea; make into rolls at 5 p. m., and bake as soon as risen. In cool weather set before fire both before and after making into rolls.

BEAT BISCUIT.

To one quart flour add one teaspoonful salt, half teacupful lard and enough cold water to make very stiff dough; beat three-quarters of an hour and bake not too fast. One quart flour will make about forty biscuits.   MRS. WATKINS.

MARYLAND BISCUIT.

Mix one tablespoonful butter and one teaspoonful salt into a quart of flour, work in milk enough to make a stiff dough, beat dough with mallet or potato masher five hundred times.

BAKING POWDER BISCUIT.

Sift through one quart flour four teaspoonfuls Royal Baking Powder and one scant teaspoonful of salt, one small tablespoonful lard, add enough milk to make soft dough.

MUSH BISCUIT.

Take quart warm mush, have some sifted flour in a pan, put mush in center, work in tablespoonful each of lard and white sugar, one teaspoonful salt, half teaspoonful soda and half cupful of yeast, mix with flour until as stiff as bread dough; let rise, work done, cut with biscuit cutter, let rise second time, then bake brown.   KENTON COOK BOOK.

TEA BISCUIT.

Two cupfuls flour, two teaspoonfuls baking powder, salt, butter size of an egg; stir all lightly. Put in enough milk to roll out soft and thin. MRS. GEO. T. DUNLOP.

BEATEN BISCUIT.

One quart flour, one teaspoonful salt, piece of lard size of an egg, same of butter, enough water and milk (half and half) to make stiff dough, knead for thirty minutes or till dough blisters, make into small biscuit, prick with fork and bake in quick oven. To make them crisp add yolk of one egg to dough.

CREAM BISCUIT.

Beat two eggs well, add a pint of cream and a large spoonful of yeast, stir in flour until the dough is stiff enough to bake, make into biscuit and set to rise for five hours. They need only a few minutes' baking. D.

LIGHT BREAD.

Two quarts flour, one teaspoonful sugar, one teaspoonful salt, half teacupful yeast, one egg well beaten, one pint water, sift flour and divide into three parts, mix one-third in batter, put one-third in jar to rise in and the other third over the batter; let it stand two hours and then work well, adding small piece of lard before baking.

CORN MUFFINS.

Three eggs beaten light, one pint buttermilk (if very sour use less), one teacupful cream or milk, one small teaspoonful soda, lard or butter size of an egg, meal enough to make batter of the consistency of pound cake batter. MRS. WATKINS.

GRAHAM MUFFINS.

One and one-half cupfuls of graham flour, one cupful of sour milk, one-half teaspoonful of soda, one egg, one-half teaspoonful of salt. Dissolve the soda in a teaspoonful of cold water, add it to the sour milk, beat the egg light, stir it into the milk and then the flour and salt. Bake fifteen minutes in quick oven. D.

VIRGINIA MUFFINS.

One quart flour, one teaspoonful salt, one tablespoonful butter and lard mixed, one tablespoonful brown sugar, one tablespoonful

BREADS.

well mashed white potato, half teacupful yeast, three well beaten eggs, rub butter and lard into flour, then potatoes, salt and sugar should be sifted with flour; pour into it the eggs and yeast and make into soft dough with cold water in summer and warm water in winter, knead half hour, make them at the same time you make light bread and the second time make into round balls without working. Grease tops of muffins, let rise two hours, then bake; the cups should be deep. MRS. GEN. GETTY.

QUICK MUFFINS.

One quart sifted flour, three eggs beaten together, one quart milk, lard size of a walnut; bake in iron gem pans; have pans hot.
MRS. DOUGHTY.

MUFFINS.

One egg beaten separately and very light, one cupful flour, one cupful milk, one teaspoonful baking powder or scant half teaspoonful soda and half cream of tartar.

GRAHAM GEMS.

One cupful milk, half teaspoonful salt, half cupful white flour, half cupful graham flour, two tablespoonfuls sugar, one teaspoonful cream tartar, half teaspoonful soda, one tablespoonful melted butter. Sift graham flour, add cream tartar, soda and white flour and sift again; mix sugar, salt and milk and stir into flour, put in the butter and drop a spoonful in each division of a gem pan, bake in hot oven for twenty-five minutes and serve hot.
MISS SKILES.

WHOLE WHEAT GEMS.

Two eggs, one-half pint of milk, one teaspoonful of salt, one and one-half cupfuls of whole wheat flour, one tablespoonful of melted butter, two teaspoonfuls of baking powder. Mix the ingredients together the same as for the flour gems and bake in hot pans for thirty minutes.

FLOUR GEMS.

One and one-half cupfuls of flour, one and one-half cupfuls of milk, one teaspoonful of butter, one egg, one and one-half teaspoonfuls of baking powder. Mix the flour and baking powder together, stir in the melted butter and the milk, and then the egg, well beaten; beat the whole until light and foamy and with it nearly fill the gem pans, which should be hot and well buttered. Bake for fifteen minutes in a quick oven. D.

CORN PONE.

Two coffeecupfuls of corn meal, one quart of milk, four eggs, one tablespoonful of drawn butter, one teaspoonful of salt and one teaspoonful of sugar. Beat the eggs thoroughly, add the meal, butter, sugar and salt and scald the whole with the milk which has been previously set on to boil. Have ready a buttered "turk's head," or, failing that, rather deep pans; pour in at once and hurry into the oven; do not let the thin appearance of the batter tempt you to add more meal, as has happened more than once when this recipe was being tried to the serious injury of the pone. The four eggs will stiffen it sufficiently, and the richness and delicacy of the cake are largely due to the small proportion of meal. The "turk's head" is preferable to the ordinary pan because the hole in the center which permits the hot air to rise diffuses the heat more equally through the mixture. Bake in a quick oven.

MRS. WATKINS.

OWENDAW CORN BREAD.

Two teacupfuls of hominy grist, and while hot mix with it a very large spoonful of butter, beat four eggs very light, yolks and whites separately, and stir them in slowly to the hominy; next add one pint of milk, gradually stirred in; lastly half pint of Southern corn meal, a little salt. Bake in a rather deep pan so as to allow room to rise. If properly mixed when cooked will be equal to a batter pudding. MISS WAGNER.

SOUTH CAROLINA CORN PONE.

Scald one pint of corn meal with boiling water, add one teaspoonful of salt, one of sugar, one tablespoonful butter, mould with the hands into oblong cakes, lay in well greased pan and bake quickly. It should be broken, not cut, and eaten very hot.

BROWN BREAD.

One pint graham flour, one pint wheat flour, mix well together and add one pint of yeast sponge, half cupful sugar, lard size of an egg, one teaspoonful salt and half pint warm water, mix as quickly and softly as possible, let rise and when light knead quickly and put in pans; when light bake. KENTON COOK BOOK.

A NEW FLANNEL CAKE.

One tablespoonful of butter, one pint of flour, one teaspoonful of salt, two eggs, two cupfuls of milk, two teaspoonfuls baking powder. Rub the butter into the flour and add the salt, beat the yolks of the eggs light, add the milk to them and when well beaten stir the milk into the flour until quite smooth, beat the whites light, add them and lastly the baking powder and bake on a hot griddle.

CORN GRIDDLE CAKES.

Six ears of uncooked corn, one cupful of milk, one cupful of flour, one tablespoonful of baking powder, one teaspoonful of melted butter, one-half teaspoonful of salt, two eggs. Grate the corn from the cob, it should measure a large pint; add the milk, salt, butter and beaten yolks of the eggs, then the flour, and lastly the beaten whites. Bake on a hot griddle, turning once and adding a little more flour if the batter is too thin. D.

FLANNEL CAKES.

One quart flour, one pint meal, one teacupful milk, one teacupful yeast, three eggs, two teaspoonfuls salt. Beat all together and let it rise until usual time in warm place.

BUCKWHEAT CAKES.

Two teacupfuls buckwheat flour, one teacupful wheat flour, three teaspoonfuls baking powder, one teaspoonful salt. Mix all together and add sufficient sweet milk or water to make soft batter. Bake on griddle at once.

WAFFLES.

One quart flour, one quart sour cream (buttermilk if you have no cream), six eggs, one and a half teaspoonfuls soda, half tablespoonful melted lard poured in after batter is mixed. This may be baked as flannel cakes or muffins.

SUPERIOR RICE WAFFLES.

One quart flour, three eggs, one cupful boiled rice beaten into the flour, one light teaspoonful soda. Make into batter with buttermilk; bake quickly in waffle irons.

OLD FASHIONED EGG BREAD.

One pint milk, three eggs well beaten, one teaspoonful salt, one tablespoonful melted butter; add enough sweet milk to make a rather thin batter; bake quickly.

BATTER BREAD.

One cupful meal, one cupful sweet milk, one cupful buttermilk, two eggs, one tablespoonful butter, one tablespoonful flour, half teaspoonful salt and same of soda.

VIRGINIA ASH CAKE.

Add teaspoonful salt to quart sifted corn meal, make up with water and knead well, make into round, flat cakes, sweep a clean place on hottest part of the hearth, put cakes on it and cover with hot wood ashes, wash and wipe it dry before eating. Sometimes a cabbage leaf is placed under it and one over it before baking, in which case it must not be washed.. MRS. WATKINS.

CORN BREAD.

One pint corn meal scalded, half pint milk, two eggs, tablespoonful baking powder. MRS. McD. R. VENABLE.

GERMAN RUSKS.

One quart flour, two eggs, two cupfuls sugar, two cupfuls butter and lard mixed, two cupfuls of potato yeast, two cupfuls milk, one nutmeg. Put all ingredients in middle of flour, work well together and set to rise as loaf bread; wash rolls over with butter and sugar.

SALLY LUNN.

One quart flour, one teaspoonful salt, one tablespoonful white sugar, rub in heaping tablespoonful butter and lard in equal parts, then rub in an Irish potato mashed fine, half cupful yeast, three eggs well beaten. Make up dough to the consistency of light bread dough with warm water in winter and cold in summer, knead half hour; when it has risen light handle lightly, put into a cake mould and bake without second kneading.

MRS. WATKINS.

SALLY LUNN.

Four cupfuls sifted flour, one and a half cupfuls milk, four eggs, one and a half cupfuls sugar, quarter of a pound of butter, pinch of salt, three even teaspoonfuls baking powder.

RUSK.

One tablespoonful sugar, one and a half teaspoonfuls salt, one cupful scalded milk, quarter cup of yeast or sixth of a yeast cake, flour to make soft dough. Mix ingredients and let dough rise over night, then heat quarter of a cupful of butter, quarter of a cupful sugar and one egg together and work into the dough, adding a little flour to make it stiff enough to mould, set to rise a second time, then shape into rolls or tiny loaves, let them rise again for an hour in a warm place and bake.

SIPPETS.

Sippets are evenly cut oblongs of bread, delicately toasted. They may be served as dry toast or with broiled birds or oysters.

SNOW CAKES.

Half tablespoonful butter, one tablespoonful sugar, whites of two eggs, one and a half cupfuls flour, one saltspoonful salt, one and a half teaspoonfuls baking powder, one cupful milk. Sift flour, salt and baking powder together four times, cream butter and sugar with a little milk, then add the well beaten whites. Bake in hot, buttered pans from twenty to thirty minutes.

MISS SKILES.

SANDWICHES.

CHICKEN SANDWICHES.

Chop the chicken, mix with mayonnaise dressing, put it between thin sliced bread with a lettuce leaf.
MRS. J. MAURY DOVE.

CHEESE SANDWICHES.

Take rich cheese and mash with silver fork, say one-fourth pound of cheese, yolks of two hard boiled eggs mixed with cheese, add enough mayonnaise dressing to season well. Cut bread in thin slices and butter, spreading cheese between slices. A leaf of lettuce can be placed with cheese between bread. These sandwiches are nice served with salad.

STUFFED ROLLS.

Cut off end of roll and remove the inside, leaving only crust. Fill with a mixture of cheese, ham or chicken sandwich, cover top with small slice cut off. This is nice for picnics or a lunch for traveling.
KENTON COOK BOOK.

PATE DE FOIS GRAS SANDWICHES.

Cut bread in very thin slices, butter, then cut diagonally, making sandwiches three cornered in shape. Spread between slices paté de fois gras, with or without lettuce leaf. Caviar can be used instead of the paté de fois gras.
MRS. F. F. FIELD.

HAM SANDWICHES.

Grate one-quarter pound cold ham in bowl with one tablespoonful chopped pickle, one teaspoonful mustard, little black pepper, six dessertspoonfuls butter. Put in a bowl and stir quickly till a cream. Add ham and seasoning; mix all well together. Spread mixture on thin slices of light bread.
MRS. WATKINS.

SHRIMP PASTE.

One pint of shrimps well boiled, remove skins, be very careful to remove all pieces of shell, pound fine to a perfect paste, a tablespoonful of butter, cayenne pepper, salt, a little grated nutmeg. Put in small earthenware cups and bake; when cold pour over the tops melted butter to exclude the air. The paste will keep for a long time, and is fine as a sandwich.
MISS WAGNER.

'Phone 347.

TRADE WITH THE...

Emrich Beef Co.

..RELIABLE MEAT and PROVISION MARKETS..

13th St. and N. Y. Ave. *21st and K Sts.*
215 Indiana Ave. *1718 14th St.*
8th and M Sts. *4th and I Sts.*
2026 14th St. *3057 M St.*
5th and I Sts. *20th St. and Pa. Ave.*

MAIN MARKET AND GROCERY HOUSE..... **1306-12 32d St.**

W. C. Downey & Co... "The Portland."

Are exclusive agents for the Richard Hudnut

Perfumes and Toilet Specialties...

In Washington, D. C.

Richard Hudnut.

H. H. BROWN---Optician...

DEALER IN — Optical and Photographic Supplies—Spectacles and Eyeglasses—Eyes examined Free .. .. ..
Cameras, Dry Plates and Films, Developing and Printing for Amatuers—Free dark room .. ..

1010 F Street N. W.

THREE CUBAN RECIPES.

CREMA DE LECHE DE COCO.

Grate one cocoanut, add one cupful of water, press through a fine strainer. To the juice add an equal quantity of thick syrup (made by boiling sugar and water in proportion of one cupful of water to a pint of sugar) and six eggs beaten well. Cook over a slow fire until it thickens like custard; when cool dust with powdered cinnamon. Serve cold.

PALANQUITA DE SANTI SPIRITA.

Roast one pound of shelled peanuts until brown, skin them and grind fine like coffee. Put this in a saucepan with one pint of sugar syrup and boil until thick; roll into balls size of a large marble when cool enough to handle. Drop these balls as fast as made into a powder prepared beforehand by grinding another quarter of a pound of roasted peanuts.

FLANDES RESTAURANTE DE CARDENAS.

Beat for half an hour the yolks of eight eggs, add to them one-quarter of a grated nutmeg, eight tablespoonfuls of wine, a pinch of powdered cinnamon, six tablespoonfuls of syrup (made from boiling one cupful of sugar and a half cupful of water until thick) and six tablespoonfuls of chicken stock. Put all these ingredients into a porcelain lined saucepan, cook for half an hour or until quite thick, stirring frequently. Serve cold.

MRS. M. C. D. JOHNSON.

SALADS.

TOMATO JELLY.

One can of tomatoes or in season eight tomatoes skinned and stewed, quarter of a box of gelatine; pass tomatoes through sieve to remove seeds, etc., season with pepper and salt and add gelatine which has been previously melted in hot water. Pour into a mould and place on ice. When cold turn out, garnish with lettuce leaves and pour mayonnaise dressing over the whole. To improve appearance of it place sliced cucumber in bottom of mould.

OYSTER SALAD.

Half gallon fresh oysters, yolks four hard boiled eggs, one raw egg well whipped, two large spoonfuls salad oil or melted butter, two teaspoonfuls salt, two teaspoonfuls black pepper, two teaspoonfuls made mustard, one teaspoonful good vinegar, two good sized pickled cucumbers cut up fine, nearly as much celery as oysters cut fine. Drain liquor from oysters and throw into hot vinegar on fire, let remain till plump, not cooked, then put at once into clear, cold water; this gives them a plump look and they will not shrink; drain water from them and set away in cool place and prepare dressing. Mash yolks as fine as possible and rub into it the salt, pepper and mustard, then rub in oil few drops at a time; when all smooth add beaten egg and then vinegar, spoonful at a time. Set aside, mix oysters, celery and pickle, tossing up well with silver fork, sprinkle in salt to taste, then pour dressing over all.

TOMATO SALAD.

Take nice, firm tomatoes, take out center, fill with chopped green peppers and a little chopped apple; serve with thick mayonnaise. MRS. WATKINS.

CHICKEN SALAD.

One large chicken boiled tender, remove all skin, fat and gristle and mince into small pieces (or cut in small pieces if you prefer), cover with damp cloth to keep meat moist, cut into small pieces three stalks of celery, mix celery and chicken, add pepper, salt and celery salt to taste, make mayonnaise and mix part of it with celery and chicken, reserving enough to put on thickly over the top. Lay in nest of lettuce leaves and garnish top with olives (seed taken out) and hard boiled eggs.

LOBSTER SALAD.

Pick lobster to pieces as you do chicken, mix with celery and season. Mix with thick mayonnaise and serve on lettuce leaves with mayonnaise poured over top. Garnish as for chicken salad.

SWEETBREAD SALAD.

This salad is made in the same way. Take pair of sweetbreads, parboil and put on ice for couple of hours, remove all parts not to be used and cut into small pieces, mix with celery and mayonnaise and serve as in above salads.   MRS. F. F. FIELD.

TOMATOES WITH CELERY.

This may be served at luncheon or as a salad course at dinner. Select firm tomatoes of a good size, cut a slice from the top of each and scoop out all the seeds and soft pulp, being careful not to break the sides. Cut celery into small dice, mix it with a mayonnaise dressing, fill shells with the mixture, place a teaspoonful of the dressing on top of each tomato and serve individually on a bed of lettuce leaves, placing three or four small leaves on each plate and the tomato in the center.

CUCUMBER SALAD.

Peel the cucumbers, which should be of medium size, cut them into halves, take out the seeds and lay the sections in cold, unsalted water for one hour. When ready to serve peel ten medium sized tomatoes and chop them fine; also chop half dozen sprays of water cress. Mix the two together and add a teaspoonful of onion juice and salt and pepper to taste. Drain the cucumbers and wipe them dry on a soft cloth. Lay them on a bed of lettuce leaves and cover them with the mixture. Pour the juice of one lemon over the whole, add a tablespoonful of salad oil and serve.

SALADE A LA CARLTON.

Cut chicken into neat slices, arrange them down the center of a long dish in alternation with slices of cold ham or tongue, mask the whole with good mayonnaise and sprinkle with French capers. Arrange about this preparation a salad of lettuce mixed with beets and cucumbers, or a macédoine of cooked vegetables according to season.

BEAN SALAD.

To make bean salad string the beans, cut them through the center and boil in salted water until tender. When cold throw over them a French dressing made of vinegar, oil, pepper and salt, and, if liked, a little chopped parsley.   D.

TOMATOES AND SWEETBREAD SALAD.

Make sweetbread salad as directed: Take one dozen nice tomatoes (medium size), remove skin and cut hole in center, removing seeds, etc. Into this cavity put sweetbread salad and cover with mayonnaise.

MAYONNAISE DRESSING.

Yolks of six eggs, whites of two, dash cayenne pepper, tablespoonful mustard, quart bottle best olive oil, saltspoonful each of table and celery salt, juice of four lemons. Rub eggs (unbeaten) and mustard well together, put in cayenne and add oil, drop by drop, stirring constantly; when all the oil has been absorbed and mixture is thick and light add salt, and after, lemon juice. Mix part of the dressing with the salad and spread the rest over the top just before serving. Keep dressing in cool place until ready for use.   MRS. F. F. FIELD.

POTATO SALAD.

Cut six medium sized, cold boiled potatoes in form of dice, grate one small onion and pour over one teacupful boiling water; then add mayonnaise dressing. Three finely cut stalks of celery are an improvement and some add a little parsley.

CHEESE SALAD, OR MOCK CRAB.

One-half pound pickled shrimps, quarter pound of good old cheese, one tablespoonful salad oil, one teaspoonful each of cayenne pepper, salt and white sugar and made mustard, four tablespoonfuls celery vinegar. Mince the shrimps and grate the cheese, stir the various condiments into the cheese, adding vinegar last; let all stand together ten minutes before adding the shrimps. Garnish with lemon.

FRENCH DRESSING.

Three tablespoonfuls oil, one of vinegar, one saltspoonful salt, half saltspoonful pepper. Put salt and pepper into cup and add one tablespoonful of the oil; when thoroughly mixed add remainder of oil and the vinegar. This is dressing sufficient for six persons. Many like grated onion juice in the dressing.
KENTON COOK BOOK.

WALDORF SALAD.

Take equal parts of pippin apples and celery cut into small pieces and lay on crisp leaves of lettuce, make good mayonnaise dressing and in it mix whites of two eggs beaten to a stiff froth and pour over all. As you peel and slice apples throw into cold water to keep white. MISS SKILES.

ORANGE SALAD.

Prepare the fruit by slicing, sprinkle with a half teaspoonful of powdered cloves to each dozen of fruit, strew plentifully with sugar. Mix in a cup or bowl the strained juice of half a lemon, half a glass of sherry and one teaspoonful of orange flower water. Mix and pour over the salad and serve.

MRS. M. D. C. JOHNSON.

FRUIT SALAD.

Slice oranges and bananas very thin, sprinkle with half cupful of sugar, two tablespoonfuls sherry and one tablespoonful maraschino, and then place in refrigerator for an hour. Wine and maraschino may be omitted in favor of lemon juice.

MAYONNAISE OF CELERY.

Use only the white part of the celery. Cut it into half inch lengths, season with salt and pepper, and when ready to mix allow one-half cupful of mayonnaise dressing to each cupful and a half of celery.

SALAD DRESSING WITHOUT OIL.

Two eggs, one-half teaspoonful of salt, one teaspoonful of corn starch, one cupful of vinegar, one teaspoonful of mustard, one teaspoonful of sugar, one tablespoonful of butter, one-eighth saltspoonful of pepper. Place the mustard, salt, pepper, sugar and corn starch in a bowl, mix them well together and add the butter and the well beaten eggs, using both yolks and whites. Set the bowl in a stew pan of hot water and cook until the dressing is thick, stirring constantly. When done add the vinegar, which should not be too strong. Use when quite cold.

MAYONNAISE DRESSING.

One teaspoonful dry mustard, one and a half of salt, pinch cayenne pepper, mix well with one and a half teaspoonfuls vinegar to smooth paste, then add one raw egg, white and yolk; beat well; half pint oil, gradually beating all the time; half gill vinegar or lemon juice.   MRS. L. E. BAILEY.

SHRIMP SALAD.

Lay shrimps in cold water for couple of hours; when ready to serve make nest of lettuce leaves, upon which place shrimps and cover with mayonnaise.

SALMON SALAD.

One can salmon picked over and all bone, etc., removed. Mash salmon smooth, add two stalks of celery chopped fine and cracker crumbs, add juice three lemons and mayonnaise. Serve on lettuce leaves.   MISS FIELD.

E. J. Sacks

DEALER IN

Butter Eggs and Cheese.

323 Centre Market.

54 Western Market.

Strange, is it Not?

But True!

That Burchell's SPRING LEAF TEA at fifty cents a pound grows on the same plant at the same time with tea at twice the price!

SOLD ONLY IN HALF POUND PAPERS.

N. W. BURCHELL,

1325 F Street

WASHINGTON, D. C.

C. E. Tribby...

RELIABLE JEWELER.

3143-3145 M St. N. W.

A. M. BAER...

UP-TO-DATE CLOTHIER AND HATTER

Cor. 32d & M Sts.   Georgetown.

.. Henry White ..

935 F Street

Kranich & Bond and Everett Pianos, and Music.

Low Prices and Easy Terms.

W. T. & F. B. WEAVER

DEALERS IN   Hardware and Harness. Contractors and Machinists' Supplies

1206 and 1212 32d Street,

WASHINGTON, D. C.

Daw & Marceron...

Artistic Window Shades.
Paper Hangings
Room Mouldings

1249 32d St., Washington, D. C.

Huyler's

Fresh! Pure!! Delicious !!!

BONBONS AND CHOCOLATES
Novelties in Fancy Baskets
And Bonbonnieres Suitable for Presents.
Cor. F and 12th Streets,
Washington, D. C.

Candies carefully packed and shipped to all parts of the Country by Mail or Express

Cocoa and Chocolates *Huyler's* are unexcelled for Purity of Material and Deliciousness of Flavor. Their Pink Wrapper Vanilla Chocolate is a favorite for Eating and Drinking. Grocers everywhere.

J. T. Mitchell,

3100 M St., Georgetown, D. C.

STOVES AND RANGES.

House Furnishing Goods.

PIES AND PUDDINGS.

ORANGE PIE.

Grate the yellow peel of one large orange and mix with juice of two, add one cupful of sugar and the beaten yolks of three eggs. Beat whites to stiff froth and beat it in one cupful of milk; then mix all and bake in a puff paste.

A RICHER KIND.

Four eggs, two spoonfuls butter, one cupful sugar, all beaten to a cream with the juice and grated rind of two oranges and a half pint of whipped cream added last, all beaten together and baked in a rich paste for twenty-five minutes in moderate oven.

TRANSPARENT PIE.

One and a half pounds butter (creamed), three pounds sugar put with the butter and well beaten together, yolks twenty-four eggs, well beaten; then mixed with butter and sugar and all well beaten together. Bake slowly. Beat whites of eggs and spread over tops of pies as you wish.

POTATO PIE.

Eight large, white potatoes, half pound butter, five eggs, sugar to taste, glass of wine, half a nutmeg, juice and grated peel of two lemons. Don't add butter to potatoes until they are nearly cold.   MRS. SPENCER WATKINS.

CREAM PUFFS.

One cupful of sifted flour, one cupful of water, one-half cupful of butter, one-half teaspoonful of salt, three eggs, two tablespoonfuls of sugar. Put butter, sugar, salt and water on the fire in a large saucepan, and when the water begins to boil add the flour dry, sifting it in by degrees with the left hand, while constantly stirring with the right. Stir vigorously until the mixture is perfectly smooth—about three minutes will generally be long enough. Remove the pan from the fire, turn the batter into a bowl and set it away to cool. When cool put in the eggs, unbeaten, adding but one at a time and beating vigorously after each addition. When all the eggs are in beat the batter until it is smooth and soft, at least fifteen minutes being necessary. Lightly butter a baking pan and drop the mixture into it from a tablespoon, using a spoonful for each puff and placing the puffs an inch apart. Bake for thirty minutes in a quick oven. These puffs are to be served cold. After taking them from the oven split them open and put in the cream, for which use the following: One-half pint of milk, one egg (yolk only), one and one-half tablespoonfuls of sugar, one tablespoonful (even) of corn starch, one-half teaspoonful of salt, two teaspoonfuls of vanilla, one-half teaspoonful of butter. Place the yolk of an egg in a teacup, beat it light with a fork, and add two tablespoonfuls of the cold milk. Place the corn starch in another cup, add to it the same quantity of milk, and when the starch is well dissolved add the egg mixture. Place the rest of the milk on the fire in a small double boiler, and when it boils stir in the mixture of egg and corn starch. Let the whole boil for three minutes, add the salt, sugar and butter, remove from the fire, and when cool add the flavoring. Pour a small spoonful of the cream into the hollow of each puff, replace the top and serve. These puffs may be eaten hot without the cream, and with a strawberry sauce.

RHUBARB PIE.

Skin the stalks, cut in lengths of half an inch, fill crust with the fruit, strew thickly with sugar. Cover with top crust and bake in slow oven three-quarters of an hour.

PUMPKIN PIE.

One quart cream, one pint stewed pumpkin, six eggs, two cupfuls sugar, one cupful molasses, one nutmeg grated, one tablespoonful ginger, two tablespoonfuls cinnamon, one small teaspoonful salt, one tablespoonful flour rubbed smooth with little milk. Then stir flour in the pumpkin, add sugar, molasses, spices and salt, the eggs thoroughly beaten, the cream last. This quantity will make three pies. KENTON COOK BOOK.

WHISKEY PIE.

One cupful apples stewed and sifted, one cupful sugar, one cupful cream, quarter cupful butter, one wine glass sherry or whiskey, three eggs beaten separately and a little nutmeg. Beat sugar, butter and apples together, then add wine, milk, nutmeg and yolks in order named. Add whites last; no upper crust. Add more whiskey if you wish. MRS. BARBER.

CHOCOLATE PIE.

One pint milk, quarter pound butter, half pound sugar, eighth of a pound of flour, vanilla flavoring, half cupful grated chocolate. Boil milk and butter together, putting teaspoonful of sugar to prevent milk from sticking to bottom of saucepan; mix sugar, flour and chocolate dry; when milk boils dump at one time the above mixture in the boiling milk, stirring rapidly until it thickens. When cold add flavoring; fill deep pie plates that have been lined with thick paste.

LEMON PIE.

Two cupfuls boiling water, with four tablespoonfuls corn starch, two cupfuls sugar, half cupful butter creamed, juice and rinds of four lemons, three eggs. Put yellow of egg when nearly cold. MISS SKILES.

APPLE PIE.

Take half peck tart apples, cut in quarters and cook in small quantity of water with skin and seeds left on. Put through sifter; when cold sweeten to taste. Butter size of an egg, white of one egg beaten to stiff froth, flavor with nutmeg or lemon, put in rich crust that has been baked. MRS. DOUGHTY.

APPLE CREAM PIE.

Line pie pan with puff paste, have some apples (three medium apples for one pie) stewed or steamed until tender, place in pan, sweeten and flavor with nutmeg one pint of rich cream; pour over apples. Bake in slow oven. The cream will be thick when pie is cold.

PEACH MERINGUE.

Line pans with puff paste, fill with canned peaches cut in halves, sweeten to taste, bake fifteen minutes. Make a meringue of whites of eggs and powdered sugar, put a tablespoonful on each half peach, return to oven for a few minutes to brown slightly. Should be eaten the day it is made. MRS. HOGE.

APPLE TART.

Line a plate with plain paste and fill with pared, cored and quartered apples. Add a scanty cupful of sugar, a quarter of a cupful of water and a sprinkling of cinnamon. Bake in a moderate oven for forty minutes. When baking any fruit pie with an upper crust success depends upon retaining the juices in the cooking. To accomplish this press the two crusts together at their juncture, wet with cold water an inch wide strip of old white cotton cloth long enough to reach about the circumference of the pie, and lay this about the edge, pressing it to the upper crust and under the edge of the tin. It will adhere to both as it dries in the cooking and will form a secure binding, keeping in the juice. Remove it as soon as the pie is taken from the oven. D.

APPLE MERINGUE.

Six large apples, quarter pound butter, half pound sugar, six eggs, reserving the whites, with which make an icing; brown on top.   MISS SKILES.

PUFF PASTE.

One pound flour, three quarters of a pound butter, yolks two eggs, little salt, teaspoonful sugar, little ice water. Sift and weigh flour and put on board or marble slab, sprinkle little salt, and very little sugar over it. Beat yolks of eggs; stir into them a few spoonfuls of ice water; pour this slowly into center of flour with left hand, working it at the same time well into the mass with tips of fingers of right hand. Continue to work it, turning fingers around on the board until paste is smooth and firm. Work butter (which must be very firm), until moisture and salt are wiped out, and it is quite supple; care must be taken, however, to keep butter from getting too soft, as it would then ruin the paste. Divide into three equal parts, spread one part as flatly and evenly as possible over half the crust, turn the other over half it, folding a second time from right to left; roll this out, spread second portion of butter on half of crust, fold and roll out as before, repeating same process for third portion of butter. The paste has now been given three turns; it should be given six; turning and rolling paste after butter is in; after the first three turns, the paste should be put on the ice for ten or fifteen minutes between each of the last three turns to prevent butter getting soft. Each time before dough is folded, it should be turned half round, so as to roll in different direction each time; this makes it more even. To turn paste, hold end to rolling-pin, then roll the pin; the dough will fold loosely around it; sprinkle board with flour, then the dough can be unrolled in side direction; this prevents handling. When folded the last time, put paste on platter, cover and place on ice for half hour; then roll out at once, or as long as kept in a half-frozen state, it may be kept a day or two. Use only firm, solid butter for puff paste.
    KENTON COOK BOOK.

BROOKLYN PUDDING.

One cupful raisins, one cupful suet, one cupful molasses, one cupful milk, two teaspoonfuls yeast powder sifted in flour. Boil in mould three or four hours. Add more raisins if you wish. Eat with Cahool or Hard sauce.   MRS. A. MIDDLETON.

LEMON PUDDING.

Four eggs, leaving out the whites of two, juice of four lemons, grated rind of two, two teacupfuls sugar, two tablespoonfuls corn starch, one tablespoonful butter, four cupfuls boiling water. Beat sugar and eggs together till very light. Add butter, corn starch, juice and rind of lemons; then pour on boiling water. Put on fire until it thickens, stirring all the time. Pour in pudding dish and bake in moderate oven half hour. Remove from stove and cover with meringue of whites of eggs and two tablespoonfuls pulverized sugar. Brown in hot oven, and serve with cream. Same recipe is an excellent filling for lemon pie.
MRS. CALLAHAN.

COCOANUT PUDDING.

One pound of butter, half pound sugar, creamed together; whites eight eggs, half glass of brandy or wine, half pound grated cocoanut; bake in thin crust.

BOILED FRUIT PUDDING.

One pint milk, three eggs, one teaspoonful yeast powder, bread crumbs to make a tolerably stiff batter, half pound currants, quarter pound raisins. Boil one and a half hours. Serve with sauce.

POTATO PUDDING.

Two pounds well mashed potatoes, one and a half pounds sugar, six eggs, half pound butter, one cup milk, wineglass wine and one of brandy; or flavor with vanilla or lemon juice.
MISS SKILES.

PLUM PUDDING.

One pound grated bread, one of suet, one of raisins, two of currants, half pound citron, half pound sugar, one pint boiling milk on the bread, one nutmeg, nine eggs, one teaspoonful salt, one wineglass of wine, one of brandy. Boil six hours. Serve with sauce.   MRS. R. T. WATERS.

A NICE PUDDING.

Quarter of a pound of lady fingers dipped in wine and rolled in jelly, put in bottom of pudding dish. Make custard of one pint milk and yellow of three eggs, sugar to taste; pour over cake. Make meringue of the whites.

RUM PUDDING.

Take a twenty-five cent sponge cake, cut in slits and pour in four tablespoonfuls rum; cover with icing made of one cupful sugar, enough water to melt it; boil till thick enough to string from spoon, pour slowly into white of one egg well beaten. Decorate with conserved cherries and blanched almonds; serve with whipped cream flavored with rum.

PUDDING FROM SOLDIERS' HOME.

Boil one quart milk, stir into it three tablespoonfuls corn starch and yolks of four eggs, six tablespoonfuls sugar. Boil it well and pour into a buttered pan; bake, flavor with lemon. Beat whites of eggs well with three tablespoonfuls sugar and when pudding is cool, put it over top and set in stove to brown. Serve with S. H. pudding sauce.

APPLE BETTY.

Pare and slice apples and put in pan, first layer of apples, then layer of sugar, piece of butter, layer of bread crumbs and some powdered cinnamon till pan is filled.

SLICED APPLE OR PEACH PUDDING.

Beat six eggs light, add one pint rich milk, pare some apples or peaches, slice thin; make eggs and milk into tolerably thick batter with flour; add small cup melted butter, bake in deep dish and serve with sauce of butter, sugar and nutmeg.

MRS. SPENCER WATKINS.

PLUM PUDDING.

One teacupful molasses, one teacupful chopped suet, one of currants, one of raisins, one of butter-milk with a spoonful of soda, one tablespoonful ginger, one of ground cinnamon, nutmeg to suit taste; flour fruit before putting in batter; steam four or five hours.

CHOCOLATE PUDDING.

One quart milk, boiled with one ounce grated chocolate, sweeten to taste, flavor with vanilla. When chocolate has thoroughly dissolved, take off and let cool; when cool enough, stir in yolks of six eggs, then put in pudding dish and bake until of the consistency of baked custard. While baking beat whites of eggs to stiff froth, adding six tablespoonfuls of sugar; season with lemon, put on pudding and brown nicely.

MRS. WILLSON OFFUTT.

FIG PUDDING.

Half pound dried figs, half pound dry breadcrumbs, half pound beef suet, two eggs, and two ounces sugar. Pour hot water over figs and soak about ten minutes, until soft. Strain water, chop figs very fine, with suet, crumbs and sugar; when thoroughly mixed and well chopped, add the two eggs beaten till very light. Pour into battered mould, and let boil in a pot from four to five hours. Serve with melted wine sauce.

COTTAGE PUDDING.

Two eggs, piece butter size of an egg, nutmeg, little vanilla, pint milk, enough flour to make batter drop from spoon, two teaspoonsfuls baking powder. Serve with wine sauce.

BLACKBERRY PUDDING.

A delicious blackberry pudding is made by beating six eggs and adding a cup of milk with half a teacupful of melted butter, a pint of flour and a teaspoonful of baking powder. Mash a quart of ripe blackberries; sweeten and stir into the batter. Turn into a pudding dish; set in the oven to bake and serve with lemon sauce.

APPLE DOWDY.

To make apple dowdy, butter a baking dish and line the bottom and sides of it with thin slices of buttered bread. Fill the centre of the dish with thinly-sliced apples; grate over a little nutmeg. Mix half a cupful of molasses with half a cupful of boiling water, and pour over the apples. Sprinkle with brown sugar, and put over more buttered bread. Cover the top of the baking dish with a tin pie pan, and set in a moderate oven for two hours. When done, loosen the edges with a knife, and turn out on a dish. Serve with sugar and cream.

MRS. BRADLEY'S PUDDING.

One cupful molasses, one cupful milk, half cupful butter, enough flour to make thick batter, fruit to taste. Eat with wine sauce.   MRS. WATKINS.

TEXAS PUDDING.

Three eggs, two cupfuls sugar, one cupful sweet milk, two tablespoonfuls flour, one cupful butter, season with fresh lemon or essence of lemon and little vinegar. Bake on a crust.
                MISS VENABLE.

LEMON BUTTER.

Beat together three eggs, then beat in two teacupfuls sugar, juice and grated rind two lemons, one tablespoonful butter and half teacupful water; let simmer over fire for fifteen minutes, stirring all the time.   MRS. DAVIDSON.

JAM PUDDING.

Three eggs, one cupful sugar, half cupful butter, one cupful jam, half cupful flour, half teaspoonful soda, three teaspoonfuls sour milk, one teaspoonful vanilla, cinnamon and nutmeg to taste; dissolve soda in milk.

HUCKLEBERRY PUDDING.

One cupful sugar, one cup molasses, three eggs, half cupful butter, one nutmeg, one and a half teaspoonfuls cloves and allspice mixed, one teaspoonful soda and one of cream tartar, one quart berries; stir in enough flour to make very stiff batter; bake one hour in two square tin pans. Serve with hard sauce.
                MISS SKILES.

PLUM PUDDING.

Two loaves baker's bread, one and a half pounds each of raisins and currants, half pound citron, eight eggs, one pound suet, chopped fine, one pint milk, enough flour to make it stiff enough to allow a large spoon to stand in it; nutmeg, allspice, cloves and mace to taste; grated rind of lemon, one small bowl brown sugar, little salt.   MISS BUCKEY.

LEMON PUDDING.

One lemon, two large white potatoes boiled and mashed, three eggs, one cup sugar, one cup milk, butter size of an egg; bake in thin crust. MRS. DOUGHTY.

CUSTARD PUDDING.

Five eggs, three pints milk, one teaspoonful corn starch, small pint sugar, teaspoonful vanilla; butter very thin bread and lay on top; bake brown and when done, sprinkle with pulverized sugar. MRS. CALLAHAN.

PEACH PUDDING.

Twelve peaches pared and sliced, three eggs, half cup sugar, two tablespoonfuls corn starch wet in cold milk, one tablespoonful melted butter one pint milk. Scald milk, stir in corn starch, when it thickens remove from fire and add butter; when lukewarm add beaten yolks. Put peaches in baking dish, sprinkle with sugar, then pour over the creamy compound. Bake in quick oven ten minutes. Make meringue of whites and little sugar, spread over top and brown. Eat cold with cream.

ORANGE ROLEY-POLEY.

Make light paste as for apple dumplings, roll in oblong sheet and lay oranges (sweet ones) peeled, sliced and seeded thickly over it, sprinkle well with white sugar, grate some of the peel over it and roll up closely, folding down the ends to secure the syrup; boil in a pudding cloth or put in steamer and steam an hour and a half; serve with lemon sauce. Cherries, apple butter or currants can be used in the same way as oranges; serve them with a sweet sauce. MISS HOGE.

APPLE DUMPLINGS.

Pare a dozen good cooking apples and take out the cores. Make very light short biscuit dough, roll out half an inch thick, and cut in large rounds; put one apple in the centre of each piece; fill the space from which the core was taken with sugar, and work the dough over the apple. Arrange on a plate a little smaller than the steamer; place it in the steamer and let steam for three-quarters of an hour. Serve hot on the plate on which they were steamed. Serve with hard sauce.

APPLE TARTS.

Apple tarts may be made by taking a pint of stewed apples; strain, and mix in the yolks of six eggs, the juice and grated rinds of two lemons, half a cupful of butter with one and a half cups of sugar; beat all together, and line small tart tins with very delicate puff paste; fill with the mixture, and bake in a very hot oven for five minutes. Spread the top of each tart with meringue, and set in the oven for one minute.

APPLE SPONGE.

This is made by covering a half box of gelatine with cold water and allowing it to stand for half an hour; then pour over it half a pint of boiling water, and stir until dissolved. Press a pint of stewed apples through a sieve and mix with the gelatine; add a pound of sugar, and stir until it melts; squeeze in the juice of two lemons; turn the mixture into a tin pan; set on ice until it begins to thicken. Beat the whites of three eggs; stir into the apples; beat all together until thick and cold. Pour into a mould and set on ice to harden. Serve with whipped cream.

SAUCES FOR PUDDINGS.

SAUCE FOR BOILED FRUIT PUDDING.

Quarter of a pound of butter, one pound sugar; wine, brandy or vanilla; cream butter and sugar together, grate a little nutmeg over it. MISS SKILES.

FOAMING SAUCE.

Two even tablespoonfuls of butter, one-half cupful of powdered sugar, one egg (white), three tablespoonfuls of sherry or one tablespoonful of vanilla. Beat the butter to a cream and gradually add the sugar, then the well beaten white of the egg, and finally the flavoring. Beat well, and when the mixture is perfectly smooth set the bowl containing it in a pan of boiling water and serve when hot. D.

LEMON SAUCE.

One cupful sugar, half cupful water, rind and juice of two lemons, yolks of three eggs; beat together sugar, lemon and water for twenty minutes, beat the yolks of the eggs, put basin containing the syrup into another of boiling water, stir the yolks into this and beat rapidly three minutes. Take off fire and continue beating for five minutes. KENTON COOK BOOK.

CREAM SAUCE.

Beat one-quarter of a cupful of butter to a cream, add gradually one-half of a cupful of powdered sugar, beating all the while. Add two teaspoonfuls of wine, and when well mixed four tablespoonfuls of cream. When ready to serve the sauce put over hot water. Stir until it is smooth and creamy. Serve at once.

HARD SAUCE.

Beat one-fourth cupful of butter to a cream, add gradually one-half of a cupful of powdered sugar, stirring constantly, and beat until very light. Add the unbeaten whites of two eggs, one at a time, thoroughly amalgamating one before adding the next, add one teaspoonful of vanilla, stir until well mixed, then add liquor if used, one tablespoonful of sherry or brandy; mix well, mold, and put in the ice box to harden before using. MRS. WATKINS.

BERRY SAUCE.

The small fruits, such as raspberries, blackberries or strawberries, make most satisfactory sauce for puddings. One pint of berries, one and one-half cupfuls of powdered sugar, one tablespoonful of butter, one egg. Place the berries in a bowl, add a tablespoonful of granulated sugar and mash slightly to draw out the juices, setting the bowl in a moderate heat; beat the butter to a cream, add the powdered sugar and when thoroughly mixed add the beaten white of the egg. Add the mashed berries just before serving.

SUNSHINE SAUCE.

One tablespoonful corn starch, one-half pint boiling water, one-half cupful sugar, one egg, one-half tablespoonful butter, one teaspoonful vanilla. Moisten the corn starch in a little cold water, add the boiling water, cook for one minute and add the sugar. Pour this hot over the well beaten egg and add the butter and vanilla.

PLUM PUDDING SAUCE.

Half pound butter, one and a half pounds sugar, one pint wine; cream butter and sugar, boil wine, stir together while boiling. Season with nutmeg. MRS. R. T. WATERS.

S. H. PUDDING SAUCE.

One small cupful sugar, one egg, piece of butter size of walnut, one tablespoonful flour, two tablespoonfuls cold water; beat up all together and pour into half pint of boiling milk or water, flavor with wine or brandy. MRS. WATKINS.

WINE SAUCE.

One cupful butter, two cupfuls powdered sugar, one-half cupful wine; beat butter to a cream, add sugar gradually, and when very light add wine, which has been made hot, a little at a time; place bowl in basin of hot water and stir for two minutes.
MISS HOGE.

BEATEN SAUCE.

Beat butter to a cream, then work in the sugar, nutmeg, one egg, wine and boiling water. MRS. WATKINS.

CAHOOL SAUCE.

One and a half pints brown sugar, one pint water, one tablespoonful butter, yolks two eggs, one nutmeg grated. Pour water, boiling, over sugar, and boil until it becomes a rich syrup, then put in butter and nutmeg, and pour the mixture over the yolks of the eggs (well beaten), stirring all the while; then replace it over the fire and stir till it thickens. Eat while hot.
MRS. A. MIDDLETON.

JAM PUDDING JUICE.

One cupful sugar, half cupful butter, one egg, three tablespoonfuls of boiling water. MISS SKILES.

RASPBERRY SAUCE.

The peel of one lemon, one cupful raspberry juice, one tablespoonful sugar, one-third teaspoonful cinnamon, one cupful water, two teaspoonfuls corn starch. Boil the lemon peel, sugar, spice and water together for five minutes, mix the corn starch with two tablespoonfuls of water, add it to the boiling water, boil for one minute, remove the lemon peel, add the raspberry juice and serve either hot or cold, as preferred.

JOHN H. MAGRUDER & CO.

Fine Groceries, Wines & Cigars

TWO STORES

1117 New York Avenue   Connecticut Avenue and M Street

W. Nordlinger ..

Popular and Reliable Clothier and Furnisher...

3107 and 3109 M Street N. W.—Washington.

ESTABLISHED 1862

Wm. H. McKnew

"Specialty Furnishing House"

Furnishings for Men and Women
Cloaks, Suits and Furs

933 Pennsylvania Avenue
Washington, D. C.

JOHN F. ELLIS & CO.
937 Pennsylvania Avenue

Pianos : Organs : Music

Musical Instruments of all kinds.

DESSERTS.

WINE JELLY.

To one package gelatine add one pint cold water, juice and peels, cut thin, of three lemons; let stand one hour, then add one quart boiling water, one pint sherry, one and a half pounds sugar; when sugar has dissolved strain and set away.

MRS. A. MIDDLETON.

COMPOTE OF PEACHES.

To make a compote of peaches, cut pared ones in halves, put in the saucepan, allow them to become heated through in their own juice, with four tablespoonfuls of sugar sprinkled over. Moisten one tablespoonful of corn starch with cold water, add two tablespoonfuls lemon juice and one egg very lightly whipped. Put the peaches on squares of sponge cake, hollow side up. Take the syrup of their juice and mix the corn starch, etc., in it. Place on stove and allow them to bubble up together, and when slightly cooled pour over the peaches; put in a cold place. The syrup will jelly all about the fruit and form a delicious dessert. Serve with plain cream. This may be prepared an hour or two before dinner.

BAKED PEACHES.

Peel a dozen large clingstone peaches, fully ripe, but firm. Stick three cloves in each, then put them in a deep baking dish with a half cupful of water, a full cup of sugar and a heaping teaspoonful of the best butter. Cook slowly until done, and serve either cold, with cream, or hot, as an accompaniment to roast fowl or game. Or you can make a superlative peach tapioca pudding by adding to them, when half done, two tablespoonfuls of tapioca, previously soaked twelve hours in cold water.

A VERY NICE DESSERT.

Dissolve one-half box of gelatine in one pint hot water, let stand long enough to cool a little, but not congeal; then add whites of three eggs, juice two lemons and sugar to taste. Beat all to stiff froth and pour into moulds. Serve with a custard made with the yolks of the eggs and one pint milk; season with **vanilla**.

CUSTARD WITH TOAST.

Four eggs, three pints milk, one teaspoonful corn starch, small pint sugar, teaspoonful vanilla. Butter very thin toast, lay on top and bake brown, sprinkle pulverized sugar over and serve with cream.

ICED APPLES.

Pare and core one dozen fine, firm apples, leaving them whole; place in stew pan with enough water to cover and stew till you can pierce them with a straw, then remove from fire and set in dish to cool, then fill center with currant or some other jelly and ice over as you would cake; serve in glass dish and eat with cream or custard. MRS. WATKINS.

FIG PUDDING.

One-half pound figs, one-half pound bread crumbs, six ounces moist sugar (wet sugar before weighing), six ounces beef suet, two eggs, little nutmeg, cupful milk; figs and suet to be chopped very fine; mix all together and steam in mould or steamer two hours; eat with sauce.

FLOAT.

One quart milk, one pint cream, ten eggs, four tablespoonfuls sugar, teaspoonful flavoring; whites of eggs well beaten to stiff froth, slightly cooked in scalding milk and kept in cool place till time for using. Custard of the well beaten yolks, sugar, cream and milk allowed to come to a boil; flavor when cold.

FLOATING ISLAND.

One quart new milk, yolks five eggs, five tablespoonfuls sugar, two teaspoonfuls vanilla, or bitter almond extract. Beat yolks well, stir in sugar and add hot, not boiling, milk, little at a time. Boil till it begins to thicken. When cool flavor and pour in glass dish. Before serving add teacupful whipped cream. You can make meringue of whites of two of the eggs and two tablespoonfuls powdered sugar. KENTON COOK BOOK.

ROSE CUSTARD.

One pint of milk, three eggs, one-half cupful of sugar, one-half pint of raspberry juice, one-eighth teaspoonful of salt. Heat the milk to the boiling point and pour it upon the well beaten eggs, then add the sugar and the salt. Cool until luke warm, when the raspberry juice may be stirred in. If not sufficiently colored, add a few drops of carmine. Pour into a buttered fancy mould and set in a saucepan of boiling water. Put into the oven and cook until firm. When cold turn out and serve on small plates. This makes a most attractive dessert.

COFFEE CUSTARD.

Excellent coffee custard may be made thus: Mix thoroughly, eight egg yolks with eight ounces of sugar, dilute with six custard cupfuls of boiling milk and a good cupful of black coffee, pass through a fine strainer, fill the cups and put them in a low pan with boiling water to half their height, take off the froth that may rise to the surface, cover the pan and let its contents simmer gently for twenty minutes. When the custard is well set, let it cool in the water, drain, wipe the cups and serve cold.

WHITE CUSTARD.

One teacupful of milk, one egg (white only), two teaspoonfuls of sugar, one-eighth saltspoonful of salt. Place the white of the egg in a bowl, add the sugar and salt, mixing them thoroughly, but not beating the egg. Heat the milk slightly, but not to the boiling point, and add it slowly to the egg. Stir until quite smooth, straining the mixture if the egg is not entirely dissolved in the milk. Place the mixture in two small custard cups, set them in a dish of boiling water, place in the oven, cover with brown paper to prevent the coloring of the custard, and bake in a moderate heat. A silver knife will come from the custards quite clean when they are sufficiently baked.

TAPIOCA CUSTARD.

One tablespoonful of pearl tapioca, one tablespoonful of prepared cocoanut, one-eighth saltspoonful of salt, one-half pint of milk, one egg, one-quarter cupful of sugar. Soak the tapioca over night in half a cupful of water. In the morning place it in a small granite stew pan, add the milk and set the pan in another half full of boiling water. Cook slowly until the tapioca is clear. Beat the yolk of the egg, the sugar, salt and cocoanut together, add a tablespoonful of water, and when well mixed stir this mixture into the milk. Cook four minutes, stirring all the time, then pour into custard cups. Beat the white of the egg, add a teaspoonful of the sugar, spread on top of the custard, add a sprinkling of cocoanut and brown delicately in the oven. This is a favorite dish.

VANILLA SOUFFLE.

One-half pint of milk, one tablespoonful of corn starch, two tablespoonfuls of flour, two tablespoonfuls of sugar, four eggs, one-quarter teaspoonful of salt. Place the milk on the fire in a graniteware pan set in another containing boiling water. Wet the corn starch and flour in half a cupful of water, and add to the milk when the latter is scalding hot. Stir until the liquid thickens, and then add the yolks of the eggs and the salt and sugar, and remove from the fire at once. Beat the whites of the eggs to a stiff froth, stir them into the hot mixture, pour into souffle or custard cups, set in a pan of hot water, bake in the oven for fifteen minutes and serve with Sunshine sauce.

RASPBERRY CREAM.

One and one-half pints of raspberries, two tablespoonfuls of granulated sugar, two tablespoonfuls of cold milk, one-half pint of cream, one tablespoonful of powdered sugar, one ounce of gelatine, one cupful of hot milk, one-half teaspoonful of vanilla. Place a pint of the raspberries in a bowl, add the powdered sugar and let them stand for an hour, then pass through a fine sieve. Put the gelatine into the cold milk and soak for half an hour, then add the hot milk and the granulated sugar, stir until the ingredients are melted, then set aside, and when cold add the gelatine to the raspberries. Whip the cream, flavor it with the vanilla, whisk all lightly together, and turn into a mould with a hollow center. Set in a cold place and when stiff turn it from the mould, place in the hollow the remaining half pint of raspberries which have meanwhile been sweetened and allowed to stand for an hour. All gelatine desserts are best when made the day before using.

JUNKET.

One pint of milk, two tablespoonfuls of sugar, two teaspoonfuls of Rennet wine, one teaspoonful of vanilla. Warm the milk until tepid, add the sugar and flavoring and when the sugar is dissolved stir in the Rennet wine. Turn into the serving dish, let it stand for ten minutes and then place carefully in a cold place. Serve very cold, with or without sugar and cream. Rennet costs but a small sum and makes a delicate dessert. Junket is quite solid when ready to serve, which will be in a couple of hours if left in a cold place.

BANANA CREAM.

Five bananas, five ounces of sugar, one-half pint of cream, one-half glassful of brandy, one lemon (juice only), one-half ounce gelatine. Peel the bananas, pound them in a mortar with the sugar, beat the cream to a stiff froth, stir in the bananas, brandy and lemon juice, mix well, add the gelatine dissolved in a little boiling water, gently pour into a mould, and stand in a cool place to "set." Jelly must be eaten with a fork.

BANANAS BAKED.

Peel one dozen rather green bananas, rub them over with a split lemon, place in a pan with red wine poured over them until it stand three-quarters of an inch deep. Drop in six cloves and a few sticks of cinnamon, three tablespoonfuls of granulated sugar and one tablespoonful of butter cut in bits. Bake in a quick oven until light brown. This makes a sufficient quantity for six persons. MRS. M. C. D. JOHNSON.

AMBROSIA.

Sweet oranges peeled and sliced, seeds removed, sprinkle freely with powdered sugar and grated cocoanut.
MRS. A. MIDDLETON.

BLANC MANGE.

One quart milk, one ounce gelatine, three-quarters of a cupful sugar. Soak gelatine in one cupful milk one hour before boiling, flavor with vanilla, wet mould with cold water.

NEWPORT BLANC MANGE.

To one quart milk add half box gelatine, soak two hours, add small cupful sugar and place over fire. When sugar and gelatine are mixed with the milk and it has come to a boil, remove and add one wineglassful sherry and teaspoonful vanilla. Stir while cooling to prevent cream from coming to the top; when cool pour in mould and set on ice.

GELATINE JELLY.

One box gelatine, soak in one pint cold water two hours, then add one quart boiling water, one and a half pounds sugar, juice three lemons.

CHARLOTTE DE RUSSE.

One pint cream, one cupful powdered sugar, one tablespoonful vanilla, quarter package gelatine, whites six eggs; when gelatine is dissolved in a little milk stir into the whipped cream, then add beaten whites of eggs; let gelatine cool before adding to the cream. MISS SKILES.

WHIPPED CREAM WITH MACAROONS.

Put one quart cream in a bowl, set it in a cold place, sweeten it properly and whip it with a Dover egg beater until it is thick, being careful that it does not break. If it is whipped a moment too long it may granulate, but this will not happen if the cream is perfectly sweet and not too rich. Very often cream that seems sweet to the taste has in reality begun to turn and will granulate at the last moment when whipped; it is, therefore, important to procure fresh and moderately rich cream. When the froth can be heaped in a bowl, it is well to cease whipping immediately. To a pint of cream, which can usually be properly whipped in from ten to fifteen minutes, allow six macaroons that are about two days old; roll them until they are finely crumbled, but not powdered, and stir enough of the crumbs into the whipped cream to give it a delicate brown color. Serve the cream in glass sauce dishes with the cake.

ORANGE JELLY.

To make orange jelly dissolve half a box of gelatine in half a cupful of cold water. Cut six oranges in halves, remove the pulp carefully and lay the skins in cold water. Add to the pulp the juice of two lemons, one cupful of sugar and one cupful of boiling water. Add gelatine, stir all together and strain. Dry the insides of the skins, notch the edges, fill with jelly and set in a cold place. When stiff, serve with cake.

STRAWBERRY PYRAMID.

Boil two cupfuls of rice in plenty of water until the grains can be easily crushed between the thumb and first finger, twenty minutes being usually long enough. Drain and spread a layer of rice on a serving dish, add an equal depth of strawberries and sprinkle lightly with sugar; then add a smaller layer of rice and sweetened strawberries, and so continue, making the layers smaller and smaller, until an apex is reached and all the rice and fruit is used. Sprinkle with sugar, and serve with whipped cream or milk.

STRAWBERRY GELATINE.

One-half box of gelatine, one-half pint of cold water, one-half pint of boiling water, one and one-half teacupfuls of sugar, one quart of strawberries, two lemons, one-half pint of cream. Soak the gelatine in the cold water for twenty minutes; then add the boiling water and stir until the gelatine is dissolved. Add the sugar and the juice from the lemons; then strain the whole into a measuring cup and add sufficient cold water to make one and a half pints of the whole. Wet a tin mould with cold water, and set a small jam jar in the middle to make a hollow center when finished, placing a weight inside the jar to keep it in place. Pour a fourth of the gelatine mixture into the mould and set on the ice to thicken, keeping the remainder in a warm place. As soon as the jelly sets, add a deep layer of the stemmed fruit, then pour in more of the mixture, again set on the ice, and when it thickens add another layer of the fruit and mixture until all is used. When ready to serve, put a little hot water into the jam jar and when the jelly is released from the sides remove the jar, set the mould for a moment in hot water to free the sides and turn out upon a flat serving dish. Sweeten the cream, whip it to a froth and heap it into the hollow center made by the jar.

STRAWBERRY SOUFFLE.

Place a layer of berries in a glass serving dish, sprinkle on a sifting of fine sugar, add another layer of the fruit, then more sugar, and so continue until the necessary quantity of berries has been used. Let this arrangement stand on ice for four hours, or even longer, if convenient. For one quart of berries allow the following: One pint of milk, two eggs, two tablespoonfuls of sugar, one teaspoonful of vanilla, one-half saltspoonful of salt. Make a soft custard of these ingredients, preparing it according to the directions in the preceding recipe, and set it on ice. Just before serving time whip to a froth half a pint of cream, add a tablespoonful of sugar, pour the custard over the top of the berries and place the whipped cream on top of the custard.

STRAWBERRY FLOAT.

One pint of strawberries, two cupfuls of pulverized sugar, two eggs, one pint of milk, vanilla to flavor. Crush the berries. Separate the whites of the eggs from the yolks, beat the former to a stiff, dry froth, and add the sugar. Put in the crushed berries gradually, beating all the while, until the whole is a stiff pile of rosy cream; then place in a glass dish and set on ice. Beat the yolks of the eggs in half a cupful of the milk, place the remainder of the milk on the stove in a graniteware pan set in another containing boiling water, and when the milk is hot add the beaten yolks, stir until the liquid is like thick cream, add salt, sugar and vanilla to taste, and set on ice to cool. This sauce is to be poured in serving about the frothy berries.

STRAWBERRY CHARLOTTE.

Eight lady fingers, one quart of strawberries, one-half pint of cream, two cupfuls of sugar. Mash a cupful of the berries, split the lady fingers in two, moisten them with the juice of the crushed berries, and use them to line a serving dish. Place in the bottom of the dish a layer of berries, season with fine sugar, whip the cream to a froth, add a layer of it, and then another of fruit and sugar, and so continue in alternation until all the cream and fruit is used. Place on ice and serve very cold.

STRAWBERRY SPONGE.

One-half box of gelatine, one-half cupful of cold water, one pint of boiling water, one cupful of sugar, one pint of strawberry juice, three eggs. Place the gelatine in the cold water, and let it stand for an hour; then add the boiling water and sugar, and stir until the sugar and gelatine are dissolved. When the mixture is cool add the fruit juice, strain, and set on ice; and as soon as it begins to thicken, stir well, and add the beaten whites of the eggs. Pour the preparation into a mould, let it harden, and serve the next day with sweetened milk or cream. D.

NESSELRODE PUDDING.

One cupful of French chestnuts, one cupful granulated sugar, one cupful of almonds, yolks of three eggs, one-half pint cream, one-half pound of candied fruits (mixed), one-half can pineapple (drained), one and a half tablespoonfuls of maraschino wine, two tablespoonfuls of sherry, one-half tablespoonful of vanilla sugar or one-quarter tablespoonful of extract. Remove shells from chestnuts, put them in boiling water for three minutes, then in cold water and take off skins, then boil until tender. Take one-half of them and press through a sieve. Blanch the almonds, chop fine, and then pound them. Cut the candied fruit and chestnuts into dice, pour over them the wine and let stand until ready for use. Put in a saucepan on the fire a cupful of granulated sugar and one-quarter cupful of boiling water. Stir until sugar is dissolved, then let cool slowly for five minutes to make a syrup. Beat the yolks of the eggs until very light, pour on them slowly the syrup, put on the fire, stirring constantly, until the mixture is like cream. Remove from fire and beat until cold, then add the cream, mashed chestnuts, pounded almonds, and freeze. When frozen remove the lid, add fruits, and turn freezer for another five minutes. Then put in fancy mould and pack. This can be served with whipped cream as pudding glace. This makes one quart of cream, and will serve ten persons, as it is very rich. The candied fruits can be omitted and stoned raisins used. This rule can be changed to suit one's fancy. I use a pint of milk with the cream, and think it better than to have it very rich.

MRS. D. S. EVANS.

LALLA ROOKH.

One quart cream, one pint milk, five eggs full, three-quarters of a pint sugar, third of a pint rum; boil half the liquid with eggs and sugar until it begins to thicken; add balance and rum just before freezing.

MRS. G. T. DUNLOP.

WINE JELLY FROZEN.

Let one ounce gelatine stand an hour in a pint of cold water, then add three pints boiling water, one and a half pounds loaf sugar, one and a half pints wine, juice three lemons, rind of two; stir all these ingredients and freeze before it congeals.

PLUMBIERE.

Make rich custard and flavor when cool with wine and extract of lemon; when half frozen add blanched almonds, chopped citron, brandy peaches cut up and any other brandied or crystalized fruit; make freezer full of custard and fill with fruit.

WATERMELON ICE.

Select ripe and very red melon, scrape some of the pulp and use all of the water; a few seeds interspersed will add greatly to the appearance; sweeten to taste and freeze as you would any other ice. If you wish it very light add whites of three eggs (thoroughly whipped) to one gallon of the ice just as it begins to congeal; beat frequently and very hard with large iron spoon.

LEMON ICE.

One quart water, one pound sugar, eight lemons, one tablespoonful gelatine. Boil sugar and water together and pour on gelatine, which has been dissolved in a little water.

ORANGE ICE.

One dozen oranges, juice two lemons, one quart water, one quart sugar, whites two eggs.

ICE CREAM.

One quart cream, half pound white sugar, whites two eggs. flavor to taste.

BISQUE.

To one pint custard add half pound of macaroons beaten fine with quart of cream and half pint wine. MRS. WATKINS.

LALLA ROOKH.

Five eggs, five tablespoonfuls pulverized sugar, one tumbler Jamaica rum poured on eggs and sugar, which must be beaten very light; then add three pints rich milk and freeze.
MRS. J. MAURY DOVE.

TUTTI FRUTTI CREAM.

One gallon cream, two and a half cupfuls sugar, two tablespoonfuls gelatine soaked two hours in milk (and then melted in double boiler), one tablespoonful vanilla. Add two tablespoonfuls of Sicily Madeira wine or maraschino, when partly frozen add one pound French candied fruit cut fine; use mixture of cherries, plums, apricots, pineapple, pears, strawberries and angelica root, or use home-made preserves carefully drained from syrup and cut into dice. KENTON COOK BOOK.

NOUGAT CREAM.

Six drops of pistachio extract, one-half cupful pistachio nuts, one quart of vanilla cream, one-quarter cupful of almonds, one-half cupful of English walnut meats. Shell and blanch the pistachio nuts and almonds, add the walnuts and chop very fine. Make the cream as directed in the preceding recipe, and when nearly frozen add the nuts and extract.

NEAPOLITAN OR FRENCH CREAM.

One quart of cream, two cupfuls of sugar, six eggs (yolks), one vanilla bean. Split the bean, remove the seeds and place with the cream in a double boiler. Cook as before directed, remove from the fire and strain. Beat the egg yolks until light, add the sugar and the scalding hot cream. Stir well and return to the boiler to cook until the cream begins to thicken. Take from the fire, cool and freeze.

PEACH OR APRICOT CREAM.

One quart of cream, three cupfuls of sugar, one quart of apricots or peaches. Make the cream as above directed. Pare and mash the fruit and add to the cream when frozen. Turn the crank rapidly for five minutes, then pack.

COFFEE CREAM.

One quart of cream, three ounces of Java coffee, two cupfuls of pulverized sugar. Grind the coffee coarsely, add it to the half of the cream that is to be cooked and let it come to a scald with the cream. Then strain through a cheese cloth, pressing well to extract all the strength of the coffee. Add the sugar, stir well and when cold add the rest of the cream, and freeze.

PINEAPPLE CREAM.

One quart of cream, one lemon, two and one-half cupfuls of sugar, one large pineapple. Scald half of the cream and half of the sugar as above directed, adding the remainder of the cream when cold. Peel the pineapple, dig out the eyes, cut lengthwise and remove the core. Grate the fruit, mix with it the remainder of the sugar and the juice of a lemon and stir until the sugar is dissolved. Freeze the cream, add the fruit and finish in the same way as for the peach cream.

CHOCOLATE CREAM.

One quart of cream, two cupfuls of sugar, two ounces of Baker's chocolate, one tablespoonful of vanilla, one-quarter teaspoonful of powdered cinnamon. Place the grated chocolate, half of the cream, the sugar and the spice together and scald as directed, stirring and beating until smooth. Strain through cheese cloth, and when cold add the rest of the cream and the flavoring, then freeze.

STRAWBERRY CREAM.

One quart of cream, one and one-half quarts of strawberries, three cupfuls of sugar, one lemon. Place one cupful of the sugar and half of the cream on the fire and scald as before directed. Add the rest of the sugar and the juice of the lemon to the strawberries; mash them very fine and let them stand for one hour, mashing and stirring frequently; then strain them through a cheese cloth. Add the other half of the cream to that scalded, and freeze. Then add the juice of the fruit, beat five minutes and pack.

WHITE CHERRY CREAM.

One quart of cream, two cupfuls of sugar, one quart of cherries, one cupful of water. Put the sugar into the water and when the sugar is dissolved add the stoned fruit. Simmer for fifteen minutes, then strain. Scald half the cream as before directed and when cold add the other half of the cream and freeze. When frozen add the strained fruit, beat five minutes and pack.

PHILADELPHIA CREAM.

One quart of cream, two cupfuls of granulated sugar, two tablespoonfuls of vanilla extract or one vanilla bean. Place half the cream and the sugar together and set the kettle in another containing boiling water. A farina kettle may be used for the purpose. Stir continually and gradually bring to a scald. It should cook at least ten minutes while reaching this stage, so slowly should it be heated. The cream will then look thin and blue. Take it from the fire and when cool add the remainder of the cream and the flavoring, and freeze. If the vanilla bean is used, split it in half, scrape out the seeds, add them and the shell to the cream when it is first placed upon the fire. When the cream is sufficiently cooked strain it through a coarse cheese cloth. All Philadelphia creams are made in this way, fruit or fruit flavoring being added after it is partly or wholly frozen. One quart of raw cream will more than double in bulk when frozen.

CLARET CUP.

Ten lemons, sixteen tablespoonfuls powdered sugar, three pints claret, six ponies red curicoa, three or four pints Apolinaris or soda water, one pint brandy, five pounds ice.

VICTORIA PUNCH.

Four oranges, eight lemons, one and a half quarts water, four cupfuls sugar, one and three-quarter cups Angelica or other sweet wine, half cupful rum, whites four eggs; heat or boil sugar and water together, add other ingredients and freeze. When nearly frozen beat whites to a stiff froth and add to frozen mixture; will be six quarts or more when frozen.

FROZEN FRUIT PUDDING.

Juice six oranges, add half tablespoonful sugar, one pint cream, well beaten whites three eggs, half dozen candied cherries, half cupful lady finger crumbs, one banana chopped fine, one slice citron chopped fine; mix orange juice, sugar and cream thoroughly, then add well beaten whites three eggs and gradually add fruit; put in freezer and when frozen stiff take out and serve in the orange skins in nest of green.

DESSERTS.

FROZEN FRUITS.

Strawberries, mash one quart and sprinkle with one cupful sugar; then boil one pound sugar in one quart water, when cool pour over mashed fruit. When frozen let stand two hours before using; if very sweet use less sugar on fruit. Other fruits can be used in the same way.

LEMON PUNCH.

To one gallon hot water add two pounds sugar, dissolve well, juice of sixteen lemons, strain and freeze. For orange, the juice of twelve oranges. Pineapple, juice of two lemons, four oranges, two pineapples minced very fine, and freeze. For sherbet add to either white of one egg.

LEMON SHERBET WITH GELATINE.

Soak one tablespoonful gelatine in little cold water for half hour, pour over it one pint boiling water, stirring until dissolved; add one cupful sugar, third of a cupful lemon juice, one tablespoonful brandy, strain and freeze. Use Nelson's or Plymouth Rock gelatine.   MISS SKILES.

CHAMPAGNE AND LEMON ICE.

For two-quart brick lemon ice break over it a quart bottle of champagne, and when it is half dissolved serve as frozen lemonade in punch glasses.

ROMAN PUNCH.

To make gallon: One and a half pints lemon juice, rinds two lemons grated on sugar, one pint rum, half pint brandy, two quarts water, three pounds loaf sugar. Pint bottle champagne is a great improvement; mix and freeze.   MRS. WATKINS.

Wood Mantels

Of neat and artistic design at LOWEST PRICES

Quartered Oak Doors.

Panel Wainscot.

Cherry Counters 16 to 24 inches.

Plate Glass furnished and set in place.

At THOS. W. SMITH'S Capital Park Mills... **1st. and G Sts. N. E.**

The C. J. McCubbin Co.

PLUMBERS, STEAM AND GAS FITTERS' ..SUPPLIES..

423 Tenth Street Northwest
Washington, D. C.

METALLIC ROOFING AND REPAIRING

ERNEST BETZ..

Furnaces, Ranges, Grates and Latrobes

1212 F Street Northwest,
Washington, D. C.

FOR
BEST
ICE CREAM
GO TO

· Budd's ·

510 NINTH ST.

CAKES.

FRUIT CAKE.

Eighteen eggs, beat separately and very light; one pound of flour, well sifted; one dessertspoonful of soda, sifted with flour; one pound of best butter, creamed; two pounds of stoned raisins; two pounds of currants, well washed; one and a half pounds of citron, cut not too fine; one pound of nuts, well broken; one small tumbler of brandy, and one of wine; juice of two oranges and two lemons, strained; the peels stewed in sugar and water till tender, cut up with scissors; one large nutmeg, one teaspoonful of mace, one of allspice, one of cinnamon, one of cloves, all finely grated. After putting your cake together, eggs, flour, butter and sugar, never beat it—in adding fruits—but stir in slowly and carefully till all is well mixed. Have ready one or two pans, with thickness of three or four sheets of paper in the bottom, well buttered; give the cake time to rise, then bake slowly for seven or eight hours; it must not be hurried, and you must not remove the cake until next day, giving it time to cool slowly, and shrink, as it is rich and heavy, and will become perfectly firm by that time, and there will be no danger of crumbling or breaking. MRS. COLLINS.

BLACK FRUIT CAKE.

One pound butter, one pound flour, one pound sugar, twelve eggs, two pounds raisins, two pounds currants, one pound citron, one tablespoonful cloves, one tablespoonful ginger, two nutmegs, two gills molasses, two gills brandy.
MRS. A. MIDDLETON.

FRUIT CAKE.

One pound butter, one pound and three tablespoonfuls granulated sugar, one pound flour, eleven eggs, one pound citron, four pounds raisins, three pounds currants, one and a half tablespoonfuls syrup, two wineglasses brandy, two of sherry, one heaping teaspoonful cinnamon, one of nutmeg, scant half teaspoonful cloves and of mace. Bake five hours in moderate oven.
MISS GARRISON.

ALBA'S CAKE.

One and a half cupfuls sugar, whites of four eggs, half cupful butter, two teaspoonfuls of baking powder, three-quarters of a cupful of milk, two cupfuls unsifted flour.

JUMBLES.

Four eggs, two cupfuls sugar, one cupful butter, one small teaspoonful soda; flour enough to make a dough stiff enough to roll out.

SUNSHINE CAKE.

Whites of five eggs, yolks of seven eggs, one cupful granulated sugar, three-quarters of a cupful of flour, one-third teaspoonful cream tartar.

DEVIL'S CAKE.

Three-quarters of a cupful grated chocolate, three-quarters of a cupful milk, same of granulated sugar, yolk of one egg; boil above until it thickens, flavor and let cool.

Cake part: One cupful sugar, half cupful butter, half cupful milk, two cupfuls flour, two eggs, one teaspoonful soda put in the flour dry. Stir in the chocolate part. Bake in layers. Ice with chocolate or white icing.

CHOCOLATE WAFERS.

One cupful brown sugar, one cupful granulated sugar, one cupful butter, one cupful grated chocolate, one egg, one teaspoonful vanilla, enough flour to make rather stiff (about one and a half cupfuls); roll very thin; bake quickly. MISS HOGE.

HOT WATER SPONGE CAKE.

Six eggs, two cupfuls of sugar, two cupfuls of flour, half cupful of boiling water, teaspoonful of lemon juice and grated rind of half lemon. MRS. J. N. MITCHELL.

SCRIPTURE CAKE.

One cup Butter.....................................Judges, 5-25
Two cups Sugar....................................Jeremiah, 6-20
Three and one-half cups of Flour (prepared)......I Kings, 4-22
Two cups Raisins..................................I Samuel, 30-12
Two cups Figs.....................................I Samuel, 30-12

One cup Almonds..............................Genesis, 43-11
One cup Water...............................Genesis, 24-20
Six Eggs.....................................Isaiah, 10-14
A little Salt................................Leviticus, 2-3
One large iron spoon of Honey................Exodus, 16-31
Sweet Spices to Taste........................1 Kings, 10-2

MARSHMALLOW CAKE.

Eighteen eggs (whites only), two and a quarter cupfuls of powdered sugar, one a half cupfuls of flour, two teaspoonfuls of cream of tartar, one teaspoonful of vanilla. Beat the eggs very lightly, and then cut the sugar in with a broad-bladed carving knife. Sift the flour three times, sift the cream of tartar into it, and then cut it into the eggs and sugar; beat, and add the vanilla. Bake in three cakes in deep, ungreased layer pans, putting brown paper in the bottoms, and using a quick oven. Then spread thickly between the layers and on top a filling made as follows: Boil two cupfuls of sugar with one cupful of water until it ropes. Just before taking it off put in half pound of marshmallow broken into bits to melt readily. Pour this mixture gradually into the well-beaten whites of two eggs, and beat continuously until cold.

CARAMEL CAKE.

One cupful of butter, two cupfuls of sugar, one cupful of milk, three cupfuls of flour, five eggs (whites), two teaspoonfuls of baking powder. Place the ingredients together as for plain layer cake, adding the whites of the eggs last. Bake in three well buttered tins and when done spread between the layers caramel filling made thus: One and a half cupful of brown sugar, one cupful of milk, one tablespoonful (scant) of butter, half tablespoonful of vanilla. Place the milk, sugar and butter on the fire in a saucepan set in another containing boiling water and cook until thick. Take from the fire and beat it hard until stiff. Then add the vanilla.

POUND CAKE.

Two cupfuls of butter, two cupfuls of sugar, four cupfuls of flour, twelve large eggs, one quarter teaspoonful of mace, half gill of brandy. Butter the pans and line them. Measure the sugar, flour, brandy and cinnamon. Separate the eggs, putting the whites in a large bowl and the yolks in a small one. Beat the butter to a cream, and gradually beat the sugar into it. When the mixture is light and creamy, add the brandy and mace. Beat the yolks till light, and add them to the beaten mixture. Beat the whites to a stiff froth, and stir them into the mixture, alternating with the flour. Pour the butter into the pans, and bake in a moderate oven for about fifty minutes.

For two loaves of raisin cake, use: One large cupful of butter, one cupful of milk, five eggs, two nutmegs, two cupfuls of sugar, four generous cupfuls of flour, one gill of brandy, half teaspoonful of soda, one quart of boiled raisins. Put the raisins in a small stew-pan, and cover them with cold water. Cook them slowly for half an hour, then drain and cool them. Beat the butter to a cream and beat the sugar into it; add the brandy and nutmeg, and beat a little longer. Add the yolks of the eggs, well beaten. Dissolve the soda in the milk, and add this to the beaten ingredients. Now add the flour. Stir in the well-beaten whites of the eggs. Spread the batter in thin layers in two large cake pans, and sprinkle raisins upon each layer. Continue this until all the materials are used. Bake for two hours in a moderate oven. This cake keeps well.

SNOW CAKE.

One pound of arrow root (ground), half pound of sugar, half pound of butter, whites of seven eggs, flavoring of essence of lemon. Beat the sugar and butter to a cream; then add the arrow root, which has been sifted; when well mixed, stir in the whites of the eggs whisked to a very stiff froth, and essence of lemon to suit the taste; again whisk the mixture for nearly half an hour; place a piece of buttered paper around the sides of the tin, and bake in a moderately heated oven.   D.

JAM CAKE.

Twelve eggs, four cupfuls of sugar, four cupfuls of flour, four cupfuls of jam, three cupfuls of butter, two teaspoonfuls of soda dissolved in water, two grated nutmegs, allspice and cinnamon to taste.

CHOCOLATE CAKE.

Two cupfuls of sugar, one of butter, two and a half of flour (sift four times), half cupful sweet milk, yolks four eggs, whites of two, ten teaspoonsfuls baking powder, two-thirds cake of chocolate dissolved in half cupful boiling water; when cool stir in batter.

ICE CREAM FILLING.

Dissolve four cupfuls of sugar in one cupful hot water, boil till it will crack when tried in glass of cold water; have whites of four eggs beaten rather stiff; pour the boiling preparation over the eggs, slowly, beating all the time. When it begins to get firm, spread on thickly on the layers of white cake, or alternate white cake and chocolate cake. If you want to use marshmallows, use same dressing between the cake and cut the marshmallows in two and place on top of dressing. Conserved cherries are used in same way.

WHITE CAKE.

Ten eggs (whites) beaten to a stiff froth, three cups of flour, one cupful of butter, two cupfuls of sugar, two teaspoonfuls of baking powder half cupful of sweet milk, one teaspoonful of vanilla. Cream the butter nicely, add the sugar and beat well; then add one-half of the half cup of milk, leaving the other for the baking powder. Add two cupfuls of flour, one at a time and beat well; then add half of your eggs, then your last cup of flour and the milk with the two teaspoonfuls of baking powder in it; then your remaining eggs. Sift the flour four times. To make pink cake, take half of your above batter and mix two tablespoonfuls of red sugar or cochineal.

MRS. WILLSON OFFUTT.

BOILED ICING.

Boil one pound granulated sugar and one small cupful of water together till a thick syrup is formed. Test this by dropping some in cold water on a plate; when done it will form like jelly in the water. Beat whites of two eggs very light and then beat in the boiling syrup gradually. Flavor to taste and beat till nearly cold. Drop spoonful on the cake and when they cool without running, apply the rest quickly. A good basis for icing to be put between layer cakes is made by boiling one cupful of sugar and half cupful sweet milk together till it is of the consistency of above icing. Flavor to taste and add chopped nuts, citron or stew some raisins with the sugar and milk; grated cocoanut may also be boiled with it or chocolate with vanilla. This icing should be beaten till stiff.

RIBBON CAKE.

One large cupful sugar, one small cupful sweet milk, one small cupful butter, one pint flour with one teaspoonful soda and two of cream tartar sifted together, four eggs; cream butter and sugar, add the beaten eggs, then the flour and milk alternately. Flavor with lemon or vanilla; put half the batter in two round pans and in the remaining batter put one cupful raisins, one cupful currants, teaspoonful spices, cloves and cinnamon, mixed, bake and put on plain and fruit alternately with jam between.

CREAM ROSE CAKE.

Stir into a cupful of sweet cream a pinch of soda, one cupful creamed butter with three cupfuls powdered sugar; whip with egg beater five minutes or until like whipped cream; flavor with vanilla and add five cupfuls prepared flour and frosted whites of ten eggs. Color a fine pink with fruit coloring; bake in layers.

FILLING.

One and a half cocoanuts grated, whites of four eggs whipped stiff; one and a half cupfuls powdered sugar, two teaspoonfuls rose water; heap the cake after filling with this mixture by beating in more sugar for the purpose.

COCOANUT CAKE.

Two cupfuls pulverized sugar, half cupful butter, beaten to a cream. Add half cup sweet milk, two and a half cups flour after it has been sifted, whites of eight eggs. Bake in jelly cake tins and put together with icing made by boiling half teacupful water, three cupfuls pulverized sugar till thick pour slowly over well-beaten whites of two eggs and beat all together till cool. Beat before putting on each layer. Sprinkle thickly with grated cocoanut; sift flour three times.

SUGAR CAKE.

Four eggs, two cupfuls sugar; beat together; half cupful milk, six cupfuls flour, half nutmeg, two teaspoonfuls cream tartar, one of soda.

GINGER CAKES.

Three pounds flour, half pound butter, half pound lard, one teacupful ginger, one paper cloves, one paper allspice, one paper cinnamon, one teaspoonful soda; enough molasses to work it up.

MRS. WATKINS.

LEMON CAKE.

Two cupfuls flour, two of sugar, six eggs, yolks and whites; beat separately; one cupful butter, half cupful milk, two teaspoonfuls cream tartar, one of soda.

For the jelly: Three quarters of a pound sugar, quarter pound butter, six eggs, rind and juice three lemons. Beat butter, sugar and eggs thoroughly together and set in a dish of hot water until heated, then add grated lemon rind and juice. Stir till thick enough and perfectly smooth. Put layers of jelly between cake while warm.

CAKES.

WHITE CAKE.

Whites one dozen eggs, five cupfuls flour, one cupful butter, one cupful sweet milk, two teaspoonfuls baking powder, three cupfuls sugar, flavored with bitter almonds. Make icing of three ounces grated chocolate, two and a half cupfuls pulverized sugar, moistened with sufficient cold water to make it the right consistency and flavor with one tablespoonful vanilla.

MRS. KENDALL.

DOUGHNUTS.

Two cupfuls of sugar, two cupfuls of sour milk, eight tablespoonfuls of melted butter, four eggs, one teaspoonful of salt, two teaspoonfuls of soda, two teaspoonfuls cream tartar, flour to thicken. Add the salt and sugar to the milk, and then the soda dissolved in a little cold water. Sift a little flour, stir it into the cream of tartar, and add this to the milk; then stir in the melted butter, and the eggs, well beaten. Add only enough flour to admit of rolling out the dough, turn the batter out upon a floured breadboard, and let it stand for fifteen minutes before cutting out. Roll out half an inch thick, cut out with a doughnut-cutter, and drop the cakes into very hot fat. When they are brown on one side, turn them with a spoon and brown them on the other side, and then take them out with a skimmer. Do not pierce the doughnuts with a fork, as that would allow the steam inside to escape and render them heavy. Roll the doughnuts in pulverized sugar when cold.

FRENCH CRULLERS.

Three eggs, one teaspoonful of salt, flour to thicken, three tablespoonfuls of milk, six tablespoonfuls of melted butter, six tablespoonfuls of sugar. Rub the butter, salt and sugar together, add the beaten egg and the milk and flour enough to roll out the dough. Roll half an inch thick, cut out with a very small cake-cutter having a hole in the center, and fry in hot lard.

HARTFORD ELECTION CAKE.

One and a half cupfuls of butter, two cupfuls of sugar, one and a half pint of flour, three eggs, one and a half teaspoonful of baking powder, two cupfuls of raisins, stoned, twenty drops of extract of vanilla, one cupful of currants, half cupful of citron, chopped, half cupful of lemon peel, chopped; half cupful of almonds, shredded; twenty drops of extract of bitter almonds, one cupful of milk. Rub the butter and sugar to a light cream, add the egg, and beat for a few minutes longer. Then stir in the flour and baking powder sifted together; add the raisins, citron, currants, lemon peel and almonds, extracts and milk; mix to a batter, place paper in a tin, and bake for an hour and a half in a moderate oven. D.

BROWN STONE FRUIT CAKE.

Half cupful butter, one and a half cupfuls sugar, two-thirds of a cupful sweet milk, two cupfuls flour, two eggs, two teaspoonfuls baking powder. Divide cake in half; take two squares of chocolate, half cupful brown sugar, three tablespoonfuls milk; heat milk, sugar and chocolate together till melted and when cold put with one half the cake, adding a little more flour; flavor with vanilla. These are to be baked in separate tins and put together with frosting or jelly.

LEMON CREAM CAKE.

Half cupful butter, two cupfuls sugar, one cupful sweet milk, three eggs, yolks and whites beaten separately, three cupfuls flour, two teaspoonfuls baking powder.

For filling: One cupful sugar, two tablespoonfuls butter, two eggs, grated rind and juice of two lemons; mix all together and boil till consistency of jelly; spread between layers and dust powdered sugar on top without filling.

CARAMEL ICING.

Two cupfuls brown sugar, one cupful milk, butter size of an egg, boil until it ropes.

MRS. PORTER'S CAKE.

One cupful sugar, one tablespoonful butter, rubbed together; break two or three eggs in coffee cup, beat, fill cup with milk, pinch of salt, cupful and a half of flour before it is sifted, teaspoonful baking powder.

Icing: One cupful sugar in saucepan, enough water to meet it, boil, do not stir; drop in cold water till it stiffens; stir constantly till cold, add vanilla. MRS. WATKINS.

FRUIT CAKE.

One and a half pounds sugar, one and a quarter pounds butter, fifteen eggs, two pounds raisins, three pounds almonds, blanched and sliced, one and a half pounds flour, one wineglass brandy, one and a half nutmegs, one and a half pounds citron. Flour fruit before mixing. MRS. DAVIDSON.

CAKES.

SOFT MOLASSES CAKE.

One tablespoonful ground ginger, two and a half cupfuls flour, one cupful molasses, two teaspoonfuls baking powder, half cupful butter, one cupful brown sugar, one cupful cold water. Beat all together till very light and bake in long pans.

SPONGE CAKE.

Twelve eggs, weight of eggs in sugar, half the weight in flour, juice of two lemons and grated rind of one.

MRS. A. MIDDLETON.

ANGEL CAKE.

Whites nine eggs, one and a quarter cupfuls sifted sugar, one cupful sifted flour, half teaspoonful cream tartar, pinch salt. After sifting flour four or five times, set aside one cupful, then sift and measure one and a quarter cupfuls granulated sugar; beat whites of eggs one half, add cream tartar and beat till very stiff; stir in sugar, then flour; bake in moderate oven thirty-five or forty minutes.

GOLD CAKE.

Yolks eight eggs, one cupful granulated sugar, scant half cupful butter, half cupful sweet milk, one and a half cupfuls flour, two teaspoonfuls baking powder. Beat yolks to stiff froth, put in milk, then flour and beat hard.

ICE CREAM CAKE.

White eight eggs, one cupful sweet milk, one cupful butter, two cupfuls sugar, two of flour, one of corn starch, two teaspoonfuls baking powder, mixed with the flour; cream butter and sugar, add milk, flour and corn starch, then the whites, beat very light, bake in cakes one inch thick.

Icing: Whites four eggs beaten very light, four cupfuls sugar; pour on sugar half pint boiling water and boil until clear and will candy in cold water; pour boiling syrup over beaten eggs, beat till nearly cold, then add one teaspoonful citric acid, two of vanilla. When cold spread as thick as the cake.

SCOTCH CAKE.

One pound flour, one pound sugar, half pound butter, three eggs, one teaspoonful cinnamon and little soda.

CREAM FILLING.

Make a cream sauce of one cupful milk, one tablespoonful flour, one tablespoonful butter; beat one egg with half cupful sugar and stir in the sauce slowly; cook for two minutes or until egg is done, flavor with vanilla or almond, use this for layer cakes or split a thin loaf of sponge cake in two and spread between layers.   MRS. DOUGHTY.

SILVER CAKE.

Whites twelve eggs, six cupfuls flour, three and a half cupfuls sugar, one cupful butter, one cupful milk, one teaspoonful cream tartar, half teaspoonful soda and two teaspoonfuls bitter almond.

FRENCH CAKE.

Half pound butter, ten eggs, one pound sifted flour, one pound sugar, two teaspoonfuls cream tartar, one of soda, half cupful milk.

ORANGE CAKE.

Four eggs, beat yolks very light, then add half pound granulated sugar, one tablespoonful water and juice one lemon; beat whites to stiff froth and lay lightly on yolks and sugar; sift a large size coffee cup of flour and sift the second time in the pan with the sugar and eggs, after adding one teaspoonful baking powder. Mix all together and bake in three layers.

Icing: Whites two eggs, one pound pulverized sugar, half lemon, grate all of it; juice and rind of one orange. Put icing between and on top of layers.

CORN STARCH CAKE.

One cupful butter creamed with two cupfuls sugar, one cupful milk, two of flour, one large teaspoonful baking powder, whites six eggs; mix well, then add one cupful corn starch, bake in moderate oven.

NUT CAKE.

Whites six eggs, one pound pulverized sugar, beat eggs and sugar three quarters of an hour, add one pound almonds; make in small drop cakes.

CAKES.

LEMON FILLING FOR CAKE.

Juice and grated rind of two large lemons, two eggs beaten a little, one and a half cupfuls sugar, butter size of walnut, little salt; if preferred use yolk of three eggs and white of one.

MOLASSES POUND CAKE.

Six eggs, one cupful sugar, two of molasses, one and a half of butter, one teaspoonful soda, ginger to taste, flour to make a batter as thick as pound cake.

CARAMEL FILLING.

One cupful brown sugar, quarter cupful sweet cream, one teaspoonful butter, boil all together till it threads, stirring slowly, as it boils for about eight minutes. Use for either frosting or filling.

MERINGUES.

Two ounces sugar to white of one egg, beat egg very light and fold sugar in; don't beat like frosting; bake on board inch thick; wet board and drop egg on with tablespoon; bake half hour in moderate oven; they are crisp when cold, take soft part out and you have the shell. Eight eggs make a dozen.

FIG CAKE.

Use any good layer cake recipe and bake in three layers, when done spread between the layers one pound figs chopped fine, one teacupful boiling water, half cupful sugar, stir all together over the fire and cool before putting on the cake. Ice the top; you can use one-third raisins and one-third figs.

MISS SKILES.

ICE CREAM CAKE.

One cupful pulverized sugar, half cupful butter (scant), half cupful sweet milk, one and two-thirds cupfuls flour, half teaspoonful baking powder, whites three eggs, beaten stiff and added last. Bake in two layers.

Icing: Four cups granulated sugar; put in pan over fire and pour over it half pint boiling water; boil till clear and will candy in cold water. Beat whites four eggs very light and pour over them slowly the boiling syrup; flavor and beat hard until cold and stiff, put between and on top as thick as cake layers.

MRS. JERE JOHNSON.

CHOCOLATE ICING.

Half cake Baker's chocolate, one cupful sugar, one and a half cupfuls milk, butter size of walnut; cook as you would caramels; flavor with vanilla.

BRANDY SNAPS.

Half pint molasses, half pound butter, three-quaters pound sugar, ten ounces flour, three of ginger, half ounce allspice; mix all together, drop with spoon in well-greased pans, well apart. Bake in cool oven until they stop boiling; when cool roll on sticks. Do not let them cool too much before taking from fire.
"THE WINDSOR."

CHOCOLATE CAKE.

Two cupfuls brown sugar, one of butter, two of flour, one and a half of grated chocolate, half cup sweet milk with one teaspoonful soda dissolved in it, whites and yolks four eggs; bake in jelly pans and ice with white icing.

Icing: On two cupfuls sugar pour half pint boiling water; boil (do not stir) until clear and waxy, pour this on beaten whites of two eggs; flavor with vanilla, beat until cool.

CHOCOLATE GEMS.

Beat two tablespoonfuls butter, adding carefully one cupful sugar, stir in half cupful water, one and a half cupfuls flour, beat thoroughly, add two teaspoonfuls cocoa, one teaspoonful vanilla and two eggs beaten to stiff froth. Before adding eggs, add one teaspoonful baking powder; pour them into greased gem pans and bake in moderate oven about twenty minutes.

CINNAMON ROLLS.

Put two tablespoonfuls butter in pint flour, beat one egg, add to it two-thirds cupful milk, add to flour one teaspoonful baking powder, half teaspoonful salt; now stir in egg and milk, mixing in lightly and roll into a thin sheet, spread lightly with butter, dust over four or five tablespoonfuls sugar, sprinkle with cinnamon; roll and cut into biscuits as you would cinnamon buns. Bake in moderately hot oven for thirty minutes.

DATE CAKE.

One cupful molasses, one of butter, two of sour milk, two of brown sugar, three teaspoonfuls soda, four eggs, four and a half cupfuls flour, one tablespoonful of any mixed spices, two pounds dates seeded and chopped fine, flour well before adding to cake; save some of the flour for that purpose. Bake in moderate oven.

SPICE CAKE.

Five eggs, leaving out the whites of four, two cupfuls brown sugar, half cupful melted butter, one cupful sour cream or milk, one teaspoonful soda, two teaspoonfuls ginger, two teaspoonfuls cloves, two teaspoonfuls cinnamon, two teaspoonfuls allspice, one teaspoonful nutmeg, three cupfuls flour. Use white icing.

MISS SKILES.

WHITE FRUIT CAKE.

One pound white sugar, one pound flour, half pound butter, whites twelve eggs, two pounds citron cut in thin, long strips, two pounds almonds blanched and cut in strips, one large cocoanut grated. Before flour is sifted add one teaspoonful soda, two teaspoonfuls cream tartar; cream butter as for pound cake, add sugar and beat awhile, then add whites of eggs and flour, and after beating batter sufficiently, add about one-third of fruit reserving the rest to add in layers as you put batter in cake mould. Bake slowly and carefully. MRS. WATKINS.

PHILADELPHIA CAKE.

White part: One and a half cupfuls white sugar, three-fourths cupful butter, three-fourths cupful sweet milk, one and a half teaspoonfuls Royal baking powder, whites six eggs, three cupfuls flour.

Dark part: One and a half cupfuls brown sugar, three quarters cupful molasses, yolks six eggs, three-quarters cupful butter, three-quarters cupful sweet milk, two teaspoonfuls baking powder, and one and a half tablespoonfuls cinnamon, one and a half teaspoonfuls cloves, three-quarters of a nutmeg, three and a half cupfuls of flour, one and a half cupfuls raisins, one and a half cupfuls currants; add some citron and figs chopped fine. This quantity makes two cakes, ice one with chocolate, the other with white icing. MRS. F. F. FIELD.

Fred. Stohlman

..Confectionery and Bakery..

Ice Cream
Water Ices
Charlotte
and
Fancy Cakes

1254 32d Street N. W.
Washington, D. C.

J. T. CLEMENTS

Undertaker
and
Embalmer

Tel. 1071.

1211 32d Street
West Washington, D. C.

Mayfield & Brown

SPECIALTIES—Truckers' Fertilizers, Washington Park Lawn Grass, Lawn Mowers, Dairy Supplies, Garden and Field Seeds, Tools, Brown Farm Wagons, Harness, Oliver Chilled Plows, Road Carts.

3147 M ST., WASHINGTON, D. C.

R. D. Weaver & Bros.

DEALERS IN

Beef, Lamb, Mutton and Veal

Cor. 32d St. and Dumbarton Ave.
Stalls 61 and 62 Western Market.

1325 32d Street

First
Co-operative
Building
Association

OF GEORGETOWN, D. C.

E. T. LYDDANE

Wholesale and Retail Dealer in

Groceries
Teas
Wines, etc.

1408-10 32d St.
West Washington, D. C.

PRESERVES, PICKLES AND CATSUP.

PINEAPPLE PRESERVES.

Pare carefully, shred with a fork, put three-quarters of a pound of sugar to each pound of fruit. Put sugar, with enough water to dissolve it, in kettle on fire. When syrup is formed put in fruit and let cook until clear. Take out fruit and lay on dish, let syrup cook until thick and clear, then put fruit in jars and pour syrup over it.

PINEAPPLE AND COCOANUT PRESERVES.

Peel and grate a pineapple, and to each pound of fruit add a half pound of cocoanut, according to taste. Measure for one pound of fruit, one pound of sugar. Take the sugar, add little water and the juice of pineapple if there is any left from peeling. Make a syrup of it by letting it come to a boil three times. Pour a spoonful or two of cold water into it and let it stand a moment; then skim. Put on fire again and when it has boiled up three times skim again. Put on the fruit and let boil, stirring with a wooden spoon, until you can see the bottom of the kettle. Pour into a dish and when cold, if you wish it, cut up into small squares and let them dry.

PRESERVED STRAWBERRIES.

Pound of sugar to pound of fruit, and a half cupful of water to each pound of sugar; boil sugar and water to rich syrup, drop in fruit and boil until fruit is clear and soft, take out fruit and lay on dish, boil syrup until very thick and rich, drop in fruit, let heat thoroughly, then put in jars and seal.   MRS. F. F. FIELD.

YELLOW TOMATO PRESERVES.

Peel and prick with large needle. To each pound of tomatoes take pound of sugar and small cupful of water, put sugar and water in kettle and let boil to syrup, put in tomatoes and boil until clear, take out and put on dishes for an hour. Put syrup on stove at the end of an hour and clarify with well beaten white of an egg, boil and skim well, then add the lemon sliced thin (one lemon to three pounds of fruit). Let boil until very rich and drop in tomatoes, cook a few minutes and can. If the tomatoes are too ripe they will break up. KENTON COOK BOOK.

SPICED PEACHES.

Take nine pounds of fruit, peel and halve; put four pounds of sugar, one pint good vinegar, cloves, cinnamon and mace in kettle; when syrup is formed throw in fruit, a few at a time, so that they will remain whole; when clear take out and put in more; boil syrup until very rich and then pour over fruit.

Cherries and pears are done in the same manner.

MRS. F. F. FIELD.

CUCUMBER SWEET PICKLES.

Lay cucumbers in salt and water for a week or ten days; take out and cut in slices a quarter of an inch thick, soak out salt and boil in alum water one-half hour and then in ginger tea an hour. Make syrup of one pint water, one quart vinegar, three pounds sugar to every four pounds cucumbers; flavor with cloves, cinnamon, mace. Boil all together until syrup is thick enough.

MRS. WATKINS.

BRANDY PEACHES.

Take white Heath clingstone peaches, pare and throw into cold water. For each pound of fruit take half pound of sugar, and for each pound sugar half pint water. Put sugar and water on stove, and when clarified and formed into syrup throw in peaches, a few at a time; when they can be pierced with a straw take out and put others in. When all are done put peaches in jars, and when syrup is cold take half brandy and half syrup and fill jars with this.

MRS. F. F. FIELD.

TOMATO JELLY.

Take ripe tomatoes, peel carefully, cutting out all rough places; to each pound put half pound of sugar, season with white ginger and mace, boil to stiff jelly, add enough vinegar to keep it.

GRAPE JELLY.

Pick grapes from stems; wash them. Put over fire with just enough water to prevent burning, cook a few minutes, mash gently with a silver spoon, strain, and to every pint of juice allow one pound of sugar. After juice comes to the boiling point boil twenty minutes, pour over heated sugar and stir constantly till all is dissolved; fill jelly glasses. MRS. WATKINS.

CRAB APPLE JELLY.

Remove all signs of decay from the apples and cut into pieces, without removing seeds or skin. Allow pound of sugar to each pint of juice, unless a very tart jelly is desired, in which case three-quarters of a pound will suffice. Proceed as with any other jelly.　　　　　　　　　　　　　　　MRS. F. F. FIELD.

ORANGE MARMALADE.

Cut one dozen oranges into thin slices, rind and all; have slices running towards the core, but do not use either seeds or core. Pour over the oranges five quarts of cold water and soak twenty-four hours. Put on to boil in same water, cook slowly three hours, add seven pounds sugar and cook slowly till tender, about four hours. Turn into tumblers, and when cold cover.
　　　　　　　　　　　　　　　　　　　　MISS SKILES.

WATERMELON RIND PICKLE.

Pare rind and cut in squares, put layer of grape leaves and then layer of rind until kettle is full; on each layer of rind sprinkle little powdered alum, cover all with water and let simmer on stove until rind is clear, then put in dishes to cool. To each pound of rind take one pound of sugar, half pint vinegar, cinnamon and cloves to taste. Boil and pour hot over rind for six mornings. The last time put rind and all on and boil till rich and clear.
　　　　　　　　　　　　　　　　　MRS. A. MIDDLETON.

CURRANT JELLY.

Pour over one peck currants on the stems one quart boiling water, let scald or boil gently till currants are thoroughly wilted. Mash and then strain through coarse muslin bag, let boil about five minutes, skim thoroughly. One pound sugar to each pint of juice; have sugar well heated and stir in juice, let come to a boil, remove scum and pour into glasses.　　MRS. GEN. GETTY.

SPANISH PICKLE.

Two dozen large cucumbers cut in large pieces, chop eight heads of cabbage, six dozen onions and two dozen green hill peppers; sprinkle all with salt and let stand all night. In the morning squeeze all out, then place in kettle in layers, alternating with the following seasonings: Four ounces white mustard seed, four ounces termeric, four ounces celery seed, four ounces black mustard, three-quarters of a pound of Colman mustard and eight pounds of sugar, well mixed with good vinegar. Have all well covered with vinegar and boil till vinegar begins to thicken.

CHOPPED CABBAGE PICKLE.

Take small head of cabbage, chopped fine, and as much celery cut in small pieces, one dozen onions, three large green peppers chopped fine, put in salt for one hour. Squeeze ingredients dry. Add three tablespoonfuls white mustard seed, one of ground mustard, sugar and pepper to taste. Cover with good vinegar and boil until thick.   MRS. SPENCER WATKINS.

CHOW-CHOW.

One quart large cucumbers cut in small pieces, one quart of coarsely cut celery, one quart of small cucumbers, one quart of small onions (white), one quart of beans and cauliflower, six green peppers. Put all in weak salt and water for twenty-four hours, then scald in same water. Six tablespoonfuls mustard, three tablespoonfuls termeric, three quarts cider vinegar, one and a half cupfuls of sugar, one cupful of flour, four teaspoonfuls of celery seed, two tablespoonfuls white mustard seed. Mix well together and cook until thick. Drain pickle well and pour paste over while boiling hot.   MRS. DAVIDSON.

MRS. SCHAAF'S TOMATO CATSUP.

Take ripe tomatoes, cut in two or three pieces and put on to boil in porcelain kettle; boil till perfectly tender, then take off to cool. When cool rub the pulp through common flour sieve to remove seeds and skin. Replace the pulp thus separated in kettle and boil down to about the consistency of starch (as prepared for laundry work). Next measure pulp, and to each three quarts add: One quart best cider (apple) vinegar, four ounces of mustard, five ounces white mustard seed, four and one-half ounces celery seed, two ounces ground cloves, one-half ounce ground cinnamon, two ounces ground ginger, two and one-half pounds granulated sugar, salt and pepper to taste. Stir frequently to prevent scorching.   MRS. MIDDLETON.

CUCUMBER CATSUP.

Grate large cucumbers, squeeze through a cloth until all juice is extracted; then add to the dry pulp celery seed, black and white mustard seed, sugar, pepper and salt to taste. Cover well with strong vinegar and put in glass jars.   MISS SKILES.

BEVERAGES.

CHOCOLATE.

Each cake is marked off into eight equal squares, each of which is an ounce. Scrape fine one ounce, mix with one ounce sugar, and add boiling water in sufficient quantity to dissolve it; then add boiling milk until the preparation reaches one pint. The beverage is now ready for use, although some persons boil it from five to ten minutes. If a lighter preparation is preferred use boiling water instead of milk. MRS. N. B. FUGITT.

BOUILLON.

Six pounds bouillion beef, cover with water, ten onions sliced, one bunch parsley; boil till soup is rich, then strain; put on ice until next day, then add yolk of one egg, boil hard for a while. Just before serving add cupful of sherry. MRS. WATKINS.

COFFEE.

The best coffee is made by mixing two-thirds Java and one-third Mocha. Allow a heaping tablespoonful of coffee and cup of boiling water for each person, also heaping tablespoonful of coffee and cupful of boiling water for the pot; settle with white of an egg, tiny pinch of salt and wet with little cold water; beat thoroughly, then add boiling water. Boil ten minutes, set back where it will keep hot, but not boil, ten minutes more.
MISS HOGE.

MILK PUNCH.

Take sweet, rich milk and sweeten to taste, add one to two tablespoonfuls best brandy, add pounded ice and shake. This is for one glassful.

CLARET PUNCH.

One bottle claret, one-quarter the quantity of ice water, three lemons sliced, three-fourths cupful powdered sugar; cover the sliced lemon with sugar and let stand ten minutes, add water, stir hard, pour in wine. Put pounded ice in each glass before filling with the mixture. KENTON COOK BOOK.

EGG-NOG.

Take half dozen eggs to each quart cream, separate eggs, beat yolks a little light, add slowly and beat in well large cupful of sugar to each half dozen eggs, add large tumbler of liquor slowly to each half dozen eggs, add little nutmeg; whip cream and beat in slowly; beat whites of eggs to stiff froth and add. Liquor should be half whiskey, quarter brandy and quarter rum.

MRS. F. F. FIELD.

RASPBERRY CORDIAL.

Put in each quart bottle one pint raspberries and six tablespoonfuls granulated sugar; then in a vessel mix alcohol and water, two cups of water to one of alcohol; fill bottles, cork and set in sun for two weeks.

MRS. JOHN G. AMES.

BLACKBERRY CORDIAL.

Put berries on and stew until well cooked up, then put in colander and let drip; afterwards put in thin muslin bag and let drip without squeezing. To each gallon of juice put three pounds sugar and put on to boil in brass or bell metal kettle, skim well; when done take off and let it get cold, then put one quart liquor (whiskey and rum) to each gallon of juice and bottle; put six cloves in each bottle of cordial. Never use anything tin about it.

MRS. A. MIDDLETON.

MINT CORDIAL.

Pick mint early in the morning while dew is on it; do not bruise it; pour some water over it and then drain off, put two handfuls in pitcher with quart French brandy, cover and let stand till next day; take out mint carefully and put in as much more, which take out the next day; add fresh mint a third time, taking it out after twenty-four hours; then add three quarts water and one pound loaf sugar to brandy, mix well and when clear bottle.

CHERRY CORDIAL.

Extract juice from ripe Morella cherries, as you would from berries, strain through cloth, sweeten to taste and when perfectly clear boil. Put gill of brandy in each bottle, cork and seal tightly. Will keep all summer in cool place. Delicious with iced water.

MRS. WATKINS.

TEA PUNCH.

Three quarts sherry, one dozen lemons (peel only), two pints sugar or more to taste, three pints green tea (quarter pound of the tea). Pour tea boiling over the lemon peel, which has been cut from lemons, and the sugar, and when cold add sherry, and, if you like it, a little rum or brandy. Delicious, and will bottle and keep for months. MRS. GEO. T. DUNLOP.

FISH HOUSE PUNCH.

Half gallon New England rum, half gallon best California brandy, three pints Jamaica rum, three dozen oranges, three dozen lemons, six pounds cut sugar, one cupful very strong tea, two quarts water. Squeeze lemons and oranges the night before and pour juice over the sugar; let stand twelve hours before mixing with liquors. Then add all other ingredients and strain through fine muslin. Grate rind of three oranges, but peel all the others before squeezing. MRS. J. MAURY DOVE.

REGENT PUNCH.

One pint strong black tea (in which put rind of four lemons cut very thin), two pounds sugar, juice six lemons, juice six oranges, one pint French brandy, one pint rum, two quarts champagne. Serve in bowl with plenty of ice.

GRAPE WINE.

Press juice carefully from grapes; to every gallon of juice add three pounds brown sugar and one quart water. Fill cask, retaining some to fill up every day during fermentation; when fermentation ceases (which will be in about six weeks) stop cask tightly and in six months rack it off and bottle.

BLACKBERRY WINE.

Fill a large stone jar with the ripe fruit and cover with water, cover and let stand three or four days to ferment, then mash and squeeze juice. To each gallon juice add three pounds brown sugar, return mixture to jar and cover closely; skim it every morning for a week till it clears from the fermentation; when clear pour carefully from the sediment into a demijohn, cork and set in cool place. When two months old it will be fit for use.
MRS. SPENCER WATKINS.

RED CURRANT WINE.

Put five quarts of currants and a pint of raspberries into a gallon of water, let them soak over night, then squeeze and break them thoroughly. Rub them well on a fine wire sieve till all the juice is extracted, washing the skins again with some of the water. Then to every gallon add four pounds of lump sugar. Bottle immediately, but do not cork, letting it work by its own fermentation. In two or three days add half a pint of brandy to every gallon of the wine, and cork as soon as the fermentation ceases.

D.

DR. McCALLA'S PUNCH.

One quart whiskey, one quart Jamaica rum, one quart brandy, two quarts strong Imperial green tea, one and a half pounds granulated sugar, one-half dozen lemons, one-half dozen oranges, one pound currant jelly, one quart bottle Apolinaris water when ready to serve with ice. Mix all water with the boiling tea after it is strained.

MR. S. M. BRYAN'S PUNCH.

One quart Jamaica rum, one quart brandy, one quart port wine, one quart strong made black tea, juice one dozen lemons, three cupfuls white sugar, one-half pint Curacao. Add equal quantity Apolinaris water with ice at time of serving. Put in sliced oranges or pineapples for flavoring.

MRS. A. MIDDLETON.

The Best Place to Buy

Lath
Shingles
Paling

THOS. W. SMITH...
CAPITAL PARK MILLS,
1ST & G STS. N. E.

R. A. CASILEAR
Real Estate, Loans and Insurance
1325 32d Street N. W.

Hugh Reilly

House and Fresco Painters' Supplies

Window and Plate Glass

1911 Penna. Avenue, Washington, D. C.
3207 M Street, Georgetown, D. C.
'Phones 1209 and 1725-3.

M. J. ADLER

Hardware •••

3148 M Street
Georgetown, D. C.

James K. Probey

Carriages
Wagons
and
Harness

1230 32d St. N. W.
Washington, D. C.

TELEPHONE 226

MANOGUE & JONES

Wholesale and Retail Dealers in

Fine Groceries

Teas, Wines, Cigars, etc.

S. E. Cor. M and 32d Sts., Georgetown, D. C.

CANDIES.

FRUITS GLACE.

One cupful granulated sugar, one cupful water, juice one lemon. Boil together for half hour. If on trying the thread of sugar, it is brittle, it is cooked enough. Divide the oranges and dry free from moisture. Pour part of the syrup in small cup, which keep in boiling water. Take the pieces of oranges (or whatever other fruit you wish to caramel) on the point of a large needle or skewer and dip into the syrup in the cup; place on a slightly buttered dish.

CRYSTALLIZED FRUITS.

Take bunches of grapes, slices of oranges, strawberries or cherries. Dip them in white of egg well beaten to a froth, and then dip them into a cup of finely powdered sugar. Lay fruit on a pan with letter paper between and set in a cool oven until the icing becomes firm, then put on a plate in a cool place.

CHOCOLATE CARAMELS.

One cake Baker's chocolate, three pounds brown sugar, one cupful milk, heaping tablespoonful butter; boil all together and when done (to ascertain this drop small quantity in ice water; if brittle, it is sufficiently cooked) take from fire, add two teaspoonfuls vanilla and beat mixture until smooth and very thick. Pour into buttered dish and when partially cool, cut into squares.
MRS. F. F. FIELD.

CREAM CHOCOLATES.

Two cupfuls sugar, one of water, two and a half of corn starch, half cake chocolate; flavor with vanilla.   MISS SKILES.

TURKISH FIG PASTE.

Weigh out four pounds of sugar, one pound glucose, nine ounces corn starch, two scruples of powdered citric acid, and have ready oil of lemon, orange or any desired extract. A few drops of red coloring fluid may also be used. Place sugar and water upon the fire, and when they come to a boil, add starch dissolved in a little cold water, and then the glucose and acid. Cook until the syrup will leave the fingers readily when tested in cold water; it is then done and should be poured out on a slab over which powdered sugar has been sifted. Smooth the top neatly and sift sugar lightly upon it. When the candy is cool, cut it into blocks and crystallize. D.

CANDIED PEEL.

Before cutting oranges for the table dip them into warm water to remove any grime on the skins and pat dry with a soft cloth; then rub the fruit with lumps of sugar to extract the oil, reserving this sugar for the final dipping. Peel the oranges and throw the skins into boiling water; cook until tender, changing the water twice. Drain well and with a pair of scissors cut into strips and weigh, allowing one pound of sugar and half a cupful of water to every pound of the peel. Boil the sugar and water together a moment then add the orange peel and simmer until transparent, which usually requires half an hour. Drain and roll each piece in the crushed sugar used to extract the oil. Lay in a warm oven or a sunny place to dry.

TO PRESERVE GINGER.

To preserve ginger, pare the roots of fresh, green ginger, using a very sharp knife, and place each piece in cold water as it is peeled. When all is peeled, drain from the water. Weigh ginger and place in preserving kettle, covering with cold water. When water is quite boiling, skim out ginger and place again in cold water. When quite cool, again return it to the kettle, add more cold water, and when boiling, skim out and lay in cold water as before. Do this three times, when the ginger will be tender, leaving it at the last in the cold water. Allow: One pound of ginger, one pint of water, one pound of sugar, one egg (white only). Place sugar and water together in preserving kettle and heat slowly, boiling slowly until sugar is dissolved. Beat white of egg until it froths, and stir into the syrup. When it boils skim until quite clear, then stand aside to cool. This is called clarifying syrup. Drain ginger, wipe dry with soft cloth and when the syrup is cold place the ginger in it and let it stand for thirty-six hours. Drain off syrup, let come to a boil, take from fire, and when again cool place in the ginger and let it remain for twenty-four hours. Drain off the syrup again, heat to boiling and this time turn over the ginger while hot. In a week again drain it off, boil it and turn it on hot. Cover closely and the ginger will be ready to use in two weeks. Preserved in this way it is a great delicacy.

CHIPS.

Mix in a kettle five cupfuls of sugar, a cupful and a half of water and a fourth of a teaspoonful of cream of tartar and set upon the fire. When the mixture boils add a fourth of a cupful of New Orleans molasses. This candy should be cooked until very hard consequently great care must be observed to prevent its burning. After the molasses has been added, the stove lid should be kept continually between the kettle and the fire, and when the candy is nearly done, the heat should be lowered, to prevent scorching. Test frequently and when a small quantity upon being dropped into water immediately becomes very hard, the candy is done and should be poured out to cool upon a well-buttered slab. When cool enough to handle pull until of a bright glossy yellow. Now place the candy near the fire, where it will keep warm, and putting on a pair of old kid gloves, pull it out into a flat strip and rub it on both sides until very thin and of a satiny appearance. Here the assistance of a second person is required to break the candy into small chips as it is pulled out and rubbed by the cook. This part of the work must be accomplished as rapidly as possible, so as to allow a minimum of time for the candy to cool. These flakes or chips may be variously colored, some with chocolate, others pink and still others pale yellow. D.

BUTTER SCOTCH.

One cupful brown sugar, one half cupful water, one teaspoonful vinegar, piece butter size of walnut. Boil twenty minutes. Flavor if desired.

MOLASSES CANDY.

One quart of molasses, one half cupful butter, one half cupful sugar. Boil and when done stir in half a teaspoonful of soda just before taking from fire.

ORANGE DROPS.

Grate rind of one orange and squeeze juice, taking care to reject seeds, add to this pinch of tartaric acid, then stir in confectioners' sugar until it is stiff enough to form into small balls the size of small marbles. Lemon juice can be used instead of orange, then leave out tartaric acid. KENTON COOK BOOK.

CREAM CANDY.

Two pounds sugar, half cupful water, two tablespoonfuls vinegar, one tablespoonful butter, boil twenty minutes, season with lemon or vanilla just as you take it off, put in dish and stir till cold.

SUGAR CANDY.

Three cupfuls sugar, half cupful vinegar, half cupful water, juice one lemon, boil (without stirring) until brittle. Pour on buttered dish and pull till light and white. MRS. WATKINS.

MISCELLANEOUS.

Cook's table of weights and measures:
1 quart sifted flour equals 1 lb.
1 quart powdered sugar equals 1 lb 7 oz.
1 quart granulated sugar equals 1 lb 9 oz.
1 pint closely packed butter equals 1 lb.
Butter size of an egg equals about 2 oz.
10 eggs equal 1 lb.
3 cupfuls sugar equal 1 lb.
5 cupfuls sifted flour equal 1 lb.
1 heaping tablespoonful equals 1-6 gill.
4 gills equal 1 pint.
2 pints equal 1 quart.
4 quarts equal 1 gallon.

SOUTH AMERICAN MARMALADE.

Take one dozen sour oranges. Cut rind into quarters and peel off; scrape all the white from rind, cover with cold water and boil till tender. Scrape skin and seeds from inner pulp, when rind is tender, cut into thin shreds and mix with juice and pulp. Add to each pint of mixture, one pound granulated sugar. Boil steadily thirty minutes.

SALTED ALMONDS.

Blanche one cupful almonds. When cold put one tablespoonful of salad oil or melted butter on them and let stand one hour, then sprinkle with one tablespoonful salt. Put them into bright baking pan in moderate oven and cook them with occasional stirring, until they are a delicate brown, about twenty minutes. Peanuts can be treated in same way.

KENTON COOK BOOK.

CHEESE BISCUITS.

Two ounces flour, two ounces butter, three ounces grated cheese, pinch red pepper and salt, yolk one egg; rub all together,

then add yolk of egg. Roll out quarter of an inch thick and cut with round pastry cutter—small.
MRS. GEO. T. DUNLOP.

CHEESE STICKS.

Pinch red pepper, quarter pound cheese, quarter pound butter, quarter pound flour, tablespoonful baking powder; work butter and flour together, then put in cheese. MRS. WATKINS.

CHEESE FONDU.

Thick slice of bread crumb into a cup of boiling milk, when well soaked strain off milk, without pressing bread, two tablespoonfuls of grated cheese, season with salt, mustard and cayenne, add the yolks of two eggs well beaten, lastly stir in the whites of three eggs well beaten, put in baking dish, dust with cracker crumb, and bake a light brown. MISS WAGNER.

CHEESE STRAWS.

Quarter pound grated cheese, two ounces flour, four ounces butter, yolk one egg, dessertspoonful mustard. Make thick paste of all the ingredients, roll it out and cut into long, narrow strips. Bake a light brown. About ten minutes will be sufficient.

TO KEEP CUT FLOWERS FRESH.

Put in vase half teaspoonful soda. To revive them take flowers from vase, throw away the cold water and replace with hot water in which you can barely hold your finger. Put in the flowers at once. The effect will be wonderful.

VIOLET PERFUME.

Half an ounce of orris root and two ounces of alcohol. Put into a bottle, cork tight and shake well.

SHRIMP PIE.

One pint of shrimps cooked and shells removed. Half pint of rice boiled very soft, while hot beat in a large spoonful of butter, two eggs well beaten, two tomatoes chopped fine, salt and pepper, in a baking dish spread a thick layer of the mixture, then one of shrimps, until the dish is full; glaze with white of egg and bake.
MISS WAGNER.

C. W. Cornwell & Bro.

Grocers

1269 32d Street N. W.
Washington, D. C.

CRAIG & JACKSON

DRY GOODS

Carpets, Mattings
and Notions

3140 M Street — Washington

J. H. VIERS...

Fine Groceries

3218 M St.— West Washington

E. L. Morgan

Fine Wines, Cigars, etc.

3059 M STREET
Washington

J. H. Buscher

510, 541 and 541½ Centre Market
9th Street Wing

Wholesale and Retail
Dealer in

Beef, Mutton, Lamb and Veal

"**If** they're Rich's Shoes
they're proper."

SEE
our $2.48 Oxfords and $3.48 Shoes
They are pretty.

B. RICH & SONS
1002 F STREET

Jarvis' Ladies' Cafe

A BRIGHT, cosy place, where ladies, unattended, may come at any time. We cater to ladies especially. Have every substantial dainty and fancy dish in season that ladies may wish for luncheon. We prepare each order separately—and serve everything in most tempting style.

JARVIS—426 9th St.
Confectioner and Caterer—'Phone 1000

JOHN T. WOOD
Dry Goods

3144 M St N. W.
Washington, D. C.

THINGS WORTH KNOWING.

If you put a piece of bread on the top of your knife when peeling onions, they will not affect your eyes, or if you peel onions under water your eyes will not cry.

To remove grass stains from white goods, wet with water, rub in some soft soap, and as much baking powder as will adhere, let stand half an hour, wash out in usual manner and the stain will be gone.

Put camphor gum with silver ware and it will not tarnish while the gum is there.

To remove ink from carpets, absorb as much as possible with a cloth, cover the spot thickly with salt, in a day or two the stain will disappear.

A piece of dry bread put into a small bag and placed in the middle of your stewpan, in which onions or cabbage are being cooked, will absorb the strong flavor.

Hartshorn will restore colors taken out by acids.

To clean straw matting, wash with weak salt water.

To test an oven for bread, pastry and other cereals not meant to rise any more, a bit of paper may be placed on it and if it turns a dark brown in five minutes the heat is just right.

An oven intended to be moderately hot for cakes, delicate puddings, etc., should burn a bit of white paper yellow in five minutes.

A six-pound roast in an oven requires one hour's roasting to be rare and an hour and a quarter to be well done.

An oven which needs to be a quick one for searing roasts before their juices escapes will in three minutes turn to a dark brown a bit of white paper placed in it.

One level teaspoonful of soda is sufficient to sweeten a pint of milk.

Four tablespoonfuls of liquid are equal to one wineglassful.

Twelve level tablespoonfuls of dry material are equal to eight that are heaped.

To prevent a bruise from discoloring apply immediately hot water, or if that is not at hand, moisten some dry starch with cold water and cover bruised place.

To remove blood stains, they can be removed from an article you do not care to wash by applying a thick paste of starch and cold water. Place in the sun and rub off in two hours; if the stain has not entirely disappeared, repeat the process.

To clean bottles, put into them fine coals, shake well, either with or without water. Charcoal left in a bottle for a little time will take away disagreeable odors.

www.ingramcontent.com/pod-product-compliance
Lightning Source LLC
Chambersburg PA
CBHW030347170426
43202CB00010B/1281